Praise for
Annibale Bugnini: Reformer of the Liturgy

"Annibale Bugnini may be the most influential liturgist of the twentieth century, whose name elicits either looks of bewilderment ("Who is he?") or passionate remonstrances. As Secretary of the Conciliar Commission on the Sacred Liturgy, his task was to help undertake the reform of the Sacred Liturgy as directed by the Second Vatican Council's *Constitution on the Sacred Liturgy*. The result radically altered the lives of all Latin-rite Christians, as well as much of the rest of the Christian West—who looked to Rome as they undertook their own liturgical revisions. This rich biography by French essayist and historian Yves Chiron is the only full-length biography of Bugnini, making this felicitous English translation by John Pepino an event of great significance. Chiron's incredible work reads like a novel and is one of the best introductions to the detailed history of the reform of the Latin rite. It is essential reading."
—FR. MATTHEW S. C. OLVER, Nashotah House Theological
   Seminary

"A lodestar in the constellation of writings concerning Archbishop Bugnini and his key collaborators in the work of the Consilium, this important biography traces key influences and events that shaped Bugnini's thinking and craft. The precision of Chiron's historical narrative helps the reader avoid exaggeration in understanding what was developmental and what was an authentic service to the will of the conciliar fathers in Bugnini's work, and it offers insight also into the objectives and desires of diverse constituencies in the preparations for the Second Vatican Council and the process of liturgical reform that immediately followed the council. Especially helpful is Chiron's meticulous documentation of the reception by the clergy and faithful of the various stages of liturgical changes, as well as his insights into the working relationship of Bugnini with Pope Paul VI. The

reader of this careful work is offered a perceptive portrait of the personalities, ideas, and events that remain central to questions surrounding the sacred liturgy even now, decades after the promulgation of the *Novus Ordo Missae*."
—JENNIFER DONELSON, St. Joseph's Seminary, Dunwoodie

"Yves Chiron's study of the life and work of Annibale Bugnini is the first scholarly work that explores the theological background as well as the personal history of a figure who, as chief architect of the post-conciliar liturgical reform, played a pivotal role in the drafting of the *Novus Ordo Missae*. Critical but always balanced, Chiron introduces us to Bugnini's early years as a Vincentian, his work for *Ephemerides Liturgicae* and the *Centro di Azione Liturgica*, as well as his initial liturgical experimentations in the 1940's such as the 'paraphrased Mass.' Chiron's study is invaluable for anyone interested in the aftermath of the Second Vatican Council and the history of the liturgical reform."
—THOMAS CATTOI, Graduate Theological Union, Berkeley

"Archbishop Bugnini will always be associated with the reform of the Roman Rite as proposed by *Sacrosanctum concilium*. Chiron's biography of this reformer combines a review of his whole life—before, during, and after the Council. As the reform continues to be a part of the ordinary life of the Church, *Annibale Bugnini: Reformer of the Liturgy* provides an important and necessary perspective."
—REV. GERALD DENNIS GILL, Rector, Cathedral Basilica of
   Saints Peter and Paul

"One often speaks about the liturgical reforms of the Second Vatican Council as if they occurred *ex nihilo*. Following the life of Archbishop Bugnini in this book—part biography, part history of the Council—we discover the very human nature, as well as the complicated history, of those reforms both before and after the Council. Even for those of us happily reared on the *Novus Ordo*, this book makes us think about the at-times messy nature of liturgical changes that have come to be the definitive

mark of the post-conciliar Church. This is an important contribution for English-speaking students of modern liturgical history."
—TIMOTHY P. O'MALLEY, University of Notre Dame

"This book is an objective presentation of the life of Archbishop Annibale Bugnini, perhaps the most significant player in the post-conciliar liturgical reform. Its greatest interest lies in the dispassionate story of his place in the post-conciliar reform, including the central role played by Pope Paul VI. Bugnini's aggressive administration of many post-conciliar commissions, especially the Consilium, eventually led to his fall from favor and exile as apostolic delegate to Tehran. An enlightening and fair treatment of a significant and interesting personality."
—WILLIAM P. MAHRT, Stanford University

"I am pleased to recommend Yves Chiron's *Annibale Bugnini: Reformer of the Liturgy*. Its peculiar merits lie in accurately describing Bugnini's often polarizing role in events surrounding the reform of the Roman liturgy. Chiron exercises the restraint necessary to provide both scholar and aficionado a clear narrative, documenting the step-by-step process of the reform with objective facts, providing a dependable summary of the Consilium's work that will be useful to any scholar in the field."
—REV. CHRISTIAAN KAPPES, Byzantine Catholic Seminary
   of Saints Cyril and Methodius

Annibale Bugnini
Reformer of the Liturgy

Yves Chiron

Annibale Bugnini

Reformer OF THE Liturgy

Foreword by
ALCUIN REID

Translated by
JOHN PEPINO

 Angelico Press

Cover design: Michael Schrauzer

CONTENTS

Foreword

by Alcuin Reid

I N 2012, thirty years after his death and one hundred years after
his birth, the autobiography of Archbishop Annibale Bugnini,
Liturgiae Cultor et Amator: Servì la Chiesa,[1] was quietly pub-
lished in Rome by his faithful secretary and executor Father Gottardo
Pasqualetti. A relatively small conference was held to mark the event.
Why did the autobiography appear only then? Why not earlier?

The answer is surely to be found in the fact that the work for
which Archbishop Bugnini is famous (or indeed, infamous, depend-
ing upon your perspective), namely the organization of the liturgical
reform following the Second Vatican Council from 1964 to 1975, was
at the time, as it remains today, highly controversial. Bugnini was a
remarkably efficient secretary and a well-connected networker. During those years he enjoyed the confidence of Pope Paul VI and had
unprecedented access to him. They worked together diligently on
the new liturgical rites that Paul VI duly promulgated to replace
those in use heretofore.

The controversy lies not in the fact that there was a liturgical
reform. There have been others in the history of the Church and
there shall, presumably, be more in the future. An Ecumenical
Council (be it Trent or Vatican II) is perfectly entitled to judge such
reform necessary. Nor does it lie in the unusual fact that Bugnini
and Paul VI worked together so closely on its detail. Rather, the
controversy lies in the assertion made by many that Bugnini orchestrated and directed the liturgical reform beyond the mandate of the
Second Vatican Council's Constitution on the Sacred Liturgy, *Sacrosanctum Concilium* (4 December 1963) so as to bring about a substantial rupture with the Church's liturgical tradition rather than an
organic development of it, as the Council had desired. In short, it is

---

1. Rome: Edizione Liturgiche, 2012.

widely held that Bugnini did what he and his circle wished to achieve, a partisan reform, rather than implementing the moderate measures authorized by the Council, and that he used his influence with Paul VI to bring about the use of papal authority to impose innovation and discontinuity.

The 2012 release of Bugnini's autobiography must, then, be seen as another attempt at influencing the judgement of history on his work. That it remains in Italian, untranslated, is unfortunate, for it contains significant historical details concerning the man and his endeavors.

This, however, is where Yves Chiron's present work, now happily available in an adept English translation, makes its first significant contribution, allowing Bugnini himself to contribute to the debate beyond the Italophone world. Of course, Archbishop Bugnini sought to define the debate with his *opus magnum*, *The Reform of the Liturgy: 1948–1975*,[2] which remains a singularly rich and primary source for any student of twentieth-century liturgical reform. Naturally Chiron draws upon this also, as well as other fundamental sources: his bibliography is a useful guide to the literature concerned.

The second contribution made by Chiron is to present the historical facts of Bugnini's liturgical involvement calmly and clearly. In a world where the internet and blogs enable and possibly even encourage any liturgical enthusiast to pontificate on this or that person or happening without regard to historical reality, Annibale Bugnini has long since been regarded by self-styled traditionalists (or hyper-traditionalists who somewhat pretentiously prefix the term with "radical") as the root of all supposed liturgical evils in the twentieth century and beyond. Such uncritical traditionalism deserves no place in serious discourse, and Chiron is careful to avoid it.

Indeed, in one frequent example of this—the labeling of the

---

2. Collegeville, MN: Liturgical Press, 1990. For critical use students must compare this English translation against the second Italian edition, corrected in many factual details by A.G. Martimort: A. Bugnini, *La riforma liturgica* (1948–1975). *Nuova edizione riveduta e arricchita di note e supplementi per una lettura analitica*, Rome: Centro Liturgico Vincenziano–Edizione Liturgiche, 1997.

reform of Holy Week definitively promulgated by Pope Pius XII in 1955 as the "Bugnini Holy Week"—Chiron is refreshingly clear that this is simply untrue. He writes: "whereas [Bugnini] played a decisive role in the Preparatory Commission [for the Council] and in the *Consilium* [to implement the Council], he did not have a leading role on the *Commissio Piana* [1948–1960]. He was an invaluable worker and rarely intervened in the discussions. He learned and observed much, probably became aware of certain problems, but never exerted a decisive influence."[3]

That is not to say that Chiron lets Bugnini off the hook. Where there is the evidence he convicts. And this is the true value of Chiron's biography: it states the case but does not overstate it. As such, it serves to advance scholarly debate and to calm the shrill cries we hear only too often in respect of liturgical reform.

And lest there be those who think that Annibale Bugnini is a much-maligned innocent, it should suffice to read his declaration at the opening of the meeting of the Preparatory Commission—of which he was the Secretary—on 11 October 1961, cited by Chiron:

> It would be most inconvenient for the articles of our Constitution to be rejected by the Central Commission or by the Council itself. That is why we must tread carefully and discreetly. Carefully, so that proposals be made in an acceptable manner (*modo acceptabile*), or, in my opinion, formulated in such a way that much is said without seeming to say anything: let many things be said in embryo (*in nuce*) and in this way let the door remain open to legitimate and possible postconciliar deductions and applications: let nothing be said that suggests excessive novelty and might invalidate all the rest, even what is straightforward and harmless (*ingenua et innocentia*). We must proceed discreetly. Not everything is to be asked or demanded from the Council—but the essentials, the fundamental principles [are].[4]

---

3. See below, p. 41. I have attempted to identify the key individuals in the Pian Reform of Holy Week in "Holy Week Reforms Revisited—Some New Material and Paths for Further Study," Alcuin Reid, ed., *Liturgy in the Twenty-First Century: Contemporary Issues and Perspectives* (London/New York: Bloomsbury T&T Clark, 2016), 234–59, at 240–41.

4. See below, p. 42.

Chiron names this "the Bugnini method." It may well lack political originality, but as this biography and indeed as other sources verify, it worked very well for Bugnini and his friends.

Bugnini's originality and maneuverability can, however, be seen in his *modus operandi* after the Council as related by Louis Bouyer, not cited herein by Chiron:

> On several occasions, whether the scuttling of the liturgy of the dead or even that incredible enterprise to expurgate the Psalms for use in the Divine Office, Bugnini ran into an opposition that was not only massive but also, one might say, close to unanimous. In such cases, he didn't hesitate to say: "But the Pope wills it!" After that, of course, there was no question of discussing the matter any further.
>
> Yet, one day when he had made use of that argument I had a lunch appointment with my friend Msgr. Del Gallo who as privy Chamberlain had a flat right above the papal apartments at the time. As I was coming back down—after the siesta, of course—and came out of the lift onto the Cortile San Damaso, Bugnini in person was emerging from the staircase on his way in from the Bronze Gate. At the sight of me, he didn't just turn pale: he was visibly aghast. I straightaway understood that, knowing me to be *notus pontifici*, he supposed I had just been with the pope. But in my innocence I simply could not guess why he would be so terrorized at the idea that I might have had an interview with the pope regarding our affairs.
>
> I would be given the answer, though weeks later, by Paul VI himself. As he was discussing our famous work with me, work which he had finally ratified without being much more satisfied with it than I was, he said to me: "Now why did you do [x] in the reform?" . . . Naturally, I answered: "Why, simply because Bugnini had assured us that you absolutely wished it." His reaction was instantaneous: "Can this be? He told me himself that you were unanimous on this!"[5]

Neither Bugnini's own words before the Council nor Bouyer's

---

5. *The Memoirs of Louis Bouyer: From Youth and Conversion to Vatican II, the Liturgical Reform, and After,* trans. John Pepino (Kettering, OH: Angelico Press, 2015), 224–25.

account here give credibility to the claim of Bugnini's autobiography, or indeed of his epitaph,[6] that he was but a humble servant of the Church.

There is more to be said, and Chiron's work moves us forward in an appreciation both of the man and his liturgical origins, and of the outline of the postconciliar liturgical reform. Other published sources should also be consulted,[7] and there is always the possibility that further archival research will shed new light.[8] To this date, the personal papers of Archbishop Bugnini are not available for consultation, seemingly closely guarded by Father Pasqualetti. A study of Paul VI's own stance (or stances) would also add an important perspective.[9]

In addition, I would like to take the opportunity to add to the historical record two observations from Bugnini's contemporaries. In May 1996 in Toulouse I interviewed Canon Aimé-Georges Martimort (1911–2000) on the postconciliar liturgical reform. In Rome in February of the same year, at the suggestion of Cardinal Ratzinger, I interviewed Alfons Maria Cardinal Stickler (1910–2007). Martimort

6. See Bugnini, *The Reform of the Liturgy*, xxii.

7. The diaries of the Secretary of the Council, Archbishop (later, Cardinal) Pericle Felici, shed light on the establishment of the *Consilium* by Paul VI and his insistence that Bugnini be its only Secretary. I explored this in my presentation to Sacra Liturgia Milan 2017 (proceedings forthcoming). See Vincenzo Carbone, *Il 'diario' conciliare di Monsignor Pericle Felice*, ed. Agostino Marchetto (Rome: Libreria Editrice Vaticana, 2015). So, too, the recently published history of the International Federation *Una Voce* sheds further light on the postconciliar period discussed herein. See Leo Darroch, *History of the Foederatio Internationalis Una Voce 1964–2003* (Leominster: Gracewing, 2017).

8. For an account of the difference between Bugnini and Paul VI on the reform of the *Ordo Missae* revealed in the *Consilium*'s internal bulletin *Res Secretariae*, see my "After *Sacrosanctum Concilium*—Continuity or Rupture?," in Alcuin Reid, ed., *T&T Clark Companion to Liturgy* (London/New York: Bloomsbury T&T Clark, 2016), 297–316, at 309.

9. The recently published work edited by Msgr Leonardo Sapienza, *Paolo VI: Una storia minima* (Rome: Edizioni VivereIn, 2018), contains some interesting remarks of Paul VI showing his surprise and even discontent with some details of the reform he himself approved in such minute detail. An earlier study, G. Simon, *Le rôle de G.B. Montini-Paul VI dans la réforme liturgique* (Brescia: Istituto Paulo VI, 1987), is not without interest; however, a new and more detailed study incorporating material that has come to light since is highly desirable.

was integrally involved in the reform from the Preparatory Conciliar Commission (1961) onward, though his personal knowledge of Bugnini predates this by many years. Stickler's involvement began with his nomination as a *peritus* of the Conciliar Liturgical Commission (1962).

Canon Martimort was the *relator* (secretary) of Study Group 9 of the *Consilium*, working on the reform of the Divine Office. The work was long, labored, and not without controversy.[10] A careful scholar, Martimort coordinated the work of his study group diligently, preparing reasoned proposals for the reform of the Divine Office which, as per the *Consilium*'s procedure, were duly discussed and voted on by its members. Bugnini, however, took a deep personal interest in the reform of the Office and often differed from Martimort in approach.

In our 1996 interview, Canon Martimort expressed his indignation that Bugnini's unprecedented (almost daily) access to Paul VI allowed him to sit through the meetings of the *Consilium* and its votes and then ignore the decisions taken by those who in fact had the authority to take them (the members) and thereby discard the months and years of work it took to achieve them, and personally take to Paul VI the proposals he himself wished to have advanced in spite of the decisions of the *Consilium* itself. In *The Reform of the Liturgy* Bugnini remarks rather smugly in respect of the reform of the Office: "the position taken by the Secretary [i.e., himself] was accepted by the Pope."[11] As a result, Martimort felt that the considerable time and effort he had put into his work had been wasted: when Bugnini wanted something in particular, neither the efforts of his so-called collaborators in the *Consilium* nor its due process were respected.

Whilst a *peritus* of the Conciliar Liturgical Commission during Vatican II, after the Council Father Alfons Stickler worked in the Congregation for Seminaries and was not directly involved in the work of the *Consilium*. His interest in the liturgical reform, however, never waned, and—by reason of his appointment during the Council itself—he was well placed to offer an assessment of its

10. See Bugnini, *The Reform of the Liturgy*, chapter 30.
11. Ibid., 511.

implementation, which he has done elsewhere and which accurately reflect our 1996 conversation.[12]

In speaking about Archbishop Bugnini, his Eminence opined: "For all the work that Bugnini did on the liturgical reform he should have been *at least* a cardinal. Instead he was removed." As Yves Chiron reports herein, allegations about Archbishop Bugnini being a Freemason surfaced after his 1975 removal from office by Paul VI and gave rise to conspiracy theories suggesting that the liturgical reform was a Masonic plot with Bugnini as its willing pawn. I therefore took the opportunity to ask Cardinal Stickler whether he believed Bugnini to have been a Freemason and whether this was the reason Paul VI dismissed him. "No," the Cardinal replied, "it was something far worse." What Cardinal Stickler believed that "something" to be, his Eminence never revealed.

Ad hominem impugnations of Bugnini's character are, of course, a distraction. Whether or not he was a Freemason or whether there was "something far worse" about his character that caused his downfall does not help us critically to examine the liturgical reform on its own merits using liturgical criteria, which is surely our real task. Demonizing Archbishop Bugnini has become a favorite pastime for some, but it is a disingenuous pastime—and one, happily, not found in the pages of this book. The liturgical reform for which Bugnini worked day and night must stand or fall on its own merits, not on his.

Indeed, it may surprise many to learn, as Chiron relates, that from his "exile" as Apostolic Pro-Nuncio in Iran, in 1976 Archbishop Bugnini made a personal intervention in the case of Archbishop Marcel Lefebvre (1905–1991), urging Rome to "continue with the weapons of exhortation, of patience, of charity, and of prayer that the Holy Father has been using so far." He continued: "In my humble opinion one must at all costs avoid a break from which it

---

12. At our meeting in 1996, his Eminence informed me that Cardinal Ratzinger "insisted" that he record his recollections for the sake of posterity. See: "Recollections of a Vatican II Peritus" in *The Latin Mass Magazine*, Winter 1999, available at http://www.latinmassmagazine.com/articles/_1999_wi_stickler.html.

would be far more difficult to return."[13] But Bugnini's intervention was too late: Lefebvre was formally sanctioned. Even more surprisingly, perhaps, some months later Bugnini proposed that the older rite of Mass be permitted by the Pope on terms similar to the 1971 Indult granted to Cardinal Heenan, Archbishop of Westminster.[14] Bugnini was, however, informed by the Secretary of State that the Pope "has asked me to communicate to you that it has not seemed opportune to grant now what has been denied in the past, and also not to worsen the confusion and disorientation by undermining the credibility of the Holy See."[15]

At the conclusion of this book, the author asks: "Did Archbishop Bugnini truly 'love' and 'serve' the liturgy? Or did he, by dint of his conception of the liturgy ... and of his constructivist will, contribute to its 'disintegration'?" Those unfamiliar with Bugnini's life and work will discover herein much with which to begin to construct an answer. Those who already know of him from what has appeared in English to date will find herein new material that will further inform and refine their opinions. And all who seek "the right way of celebrating the Liturgy, inwardly and outwardly,"[16] will gain more with which to answer the question that will simply not go away: is the liturgical reform promulgated by Paul VI a legitimate, organic development of the Church's liturgical tradition, as willed and mandated by the Second Vatican Council, or is it—to borrow another's words—"a fabrication, a banal on-the-spot product"?[17] Therefore, for all that this book enables we are in the debt of Angelico Press and indeed of Yves Chiron himself.

Dom Alcuin Reid

30 August 2018

13. See below, p. 179.

14. For discussion of the indult, see below, pp. 149–50.

15. See below, p. 180.

16. Joseph Cardinal Ratzinger, *The Spirit of the Liturgy* (San Francisco: Ignatius Press, 2000), 8–9.

17. "une fabrication, produit banal de l'instant": Joseph Cardinal Ratzinger, "Klaus Gamber: L'intrépidité d'un vraie témoin," in Klaus Gamber, *La Réforme Liturgique en question* (Le Barroux: Éditions Sainte-Madeleine, 1992), 6–8, at 8.

Author's Preface

A RCHBISHOP BUGNINI is among the most controversial characters in contemporary Church history. For some he is the architect of the boldest and most successful liturgical reform ever accomplished in the history of the Church. For others he is a ransacker of the liturgy, the man responsible for its desecration, and his very name, Annibale (Hannibal), seems like a portent of this devastation.

Hostility has been and still is so great in some quarters that falsehoods or unverified rumors circulate against him. The most common of these—which is still to be found in the recently published memoirs of another eminent liturgist—is to call him "Neapolitan," thereby insinuating a sort of congenital dishonesty. As a matter of fact he was born in the middle of Italy.

Another rumor, which has been repeated for forty years, holds that he was a Freemason. This would allegedly explain both his intention to overturn the traditional liturgy and his fall from Paul VI's favor in July 1975.

Strangely, no monograph has yet been devoted to Annibale Bugnini, whether in Italy, France, or elsewhere. His closest collaborators, Vincentian Fr Carlo Braga and Fr Gottardo Pasqualetti of the Istituto Missioni Consolata, have kept his memory alive to this day. They have published three books, all of them posthumous:

- A Festschrift edited for his seventieth birthday that came out the very year he died: *Liturgia divina e umana. Studi sulla riforma liturgica offerti a S.E. Mons. Annibale Bugnini in occasione del suo 70ᵉ compleano* (Rome: Edizioni Liturgiche, 1982), 715 pages. It is a collection of studies and testimonies published by his liturgist friends, his collaborators, and his friends.
- The big book Annibale Bugnini had been working on since 1975 and which he completed in 1981. It was only published two years later: *La Riforma liturgica (1948–1975)* (Rome: Edizioni Liturgiche, 1983), 930 pages.

- The memoirs he had completed by 1977 and which were only published on the thirtieth anniversary of his death: *"Liturgiae Cultor et Amator, Servì la Chiesa."* *Memorie Autobiografiche* (Rome: Edizioni Liturgiche, 2012), 231 pages.

While the second of these is both documentary and self-justifying, Bugnini clearly wrote the third one to defend himself.

These sources are not enough for a complete grasp of Bugnini's career or for a true understanding of his activity. Other avenues must be explored.

The Paris archives of his congregation, the Congregation of the Mission, preserve a good number of his works. I was also able to interview Fr Carlo Braga (1927–2014) in Rome; he had been Bugnini's faithful disciple. The still-unpublished letters that Bugnini wrote to Dom Adalbert Franquesa (one of the first consultors for the *Consilium*) are preserved in the Catalan abbey of Montserrat and shed some interesting light.

Also useful are the testimonies published by several liturgists whom Bugnini knew long before the Second Vatican Council and who worked with him before, during, and after the Council (Canon Martimort, Dom Botte, Fr Gy, and others).

One must also refer to the works of one of his collaborators, Piero Marini, ordained a priest in 1965. He became his secretary that very year and worked with him for ten years. Unlike Fr Braga and Fr Pasqualetti, who have been fervent disciples engaged in defending his memory to this day, Piero Marini has distanced himself from the man with whom he had worked.[1] Archbishop Marini has been depicted—improperly—as a "Bugninist." After Archbishop Bugnini had been kept off the Congregation for Divine Worship, Piero Marini remained in function in that Congregation and was later named Master of papal liturgical celebrations in 1987, a post he held until 2007, when he was named president of the Pontifical Committee for International Eucharistic Congresses.[2]

---

1. The same might be said of Cardinal Virgilio Noè, another of Bugnini's collaborators.

2. Piero Marini, *Cérémoniaire des papes* (Paris: Bayard, 2007).

While remaining strongly attached to the liturgical reform undertaken after Vatican II, in his works on the subject Archbishop Piero Marini hints at critical judgments on Archbishop Bugnini. In point of fact he is more critical of certain aspects of Bugnini's personality and methods than of his aims. Significantly, in his principal historical study of the liturgical reform,[3] Archbishop Marini nowhere refers to his "master's" lengthy book, *La Riforma liturgica*, whereas he quotes many other sources and writings of Archbishop Bugnini's.

One must also take into consideration the witness of another liturgy expert, Franciscan Father Ferdinando Antonelli. He was in turn *relator* at the historical section of the Congregation of Rites, member of the Pontifical Commission for Liturgical Reform under Pius XII, secretary of the liturgical commission of Vatican II, member of the postconciliar *Consilium*, secretary of the Congregation of Rites and then of the Congregation for Divine Worship. He spent several decades in the same commissions as Archbishop Bugnini and sometimes found himself his unwilling rival. Paul VI created him cardinal in 1973. The diary he left, which Nicola Giampietro partly edited along with other documents,[4] is a highly worthwhile source, often in counterpoint to Bugnini's testimony.

Beyond the black legend, at the end of this study of sources and witnesses Archbishop Bugnini emerges as a remarkable organizer rather than as a theologian or liturgy expert. Cardinal Antonelli, who worked beside him from 1948 on, was to jot down twenty years later in a personal work: "While I would like to be mistaken, I can say that his greatest lacuna was his lack of any theological training or sensibility. This was a grave defect and lacuna because in the liturgy, every word and every gesture expresses a theological idea."[5]

It was for other qualities that Archbishop Bugnini was esteemed at different points in his career. He was able to draw on specialists,

---

3. This work was not published in Rome, as one might have expected, but in English in the United States: *A Challenging Reform: Realizing the Vision of the Liturgical Renewal, 1963–1975* (Collegeville, MN: Liturgical Press, 2007).

4. Nicola Giampietro, *The Development of the Liturgical Reform As Seen by Cardinal Ferdinando Antonelli from 1948 to 1970* (Fort Collins, CO: Roman Catholic Books, 2009).

5. Ibid., 196.

made them work, and led the higher authority to adopt the drafts they prepared. Lastly, he was able—often at forced march—to implement a liturgical reform project which he had only played a part in conceiving. He was able to win Paul VI over to this plan, until the pope, after ten years, no longer judged him to be the man of the situation (according to the benign interpretation) or withdrew his trust from him (according to the more critical interpretation).

One sometimes reads that the Council's Constitution on the Liturgy did not call for a reform of the Mass. This is false. Article 50 of the Constitution explicitly demands:

> The rite of the Mass is to be revised [*Ordo Missae ita recognoscatur*] in such a way that the intrinsic nature and purpose of its several parts, as also the connection between them, may be more clearly manifested, and that devout and active participation by the faithful may be more easily achieved.[6]

The rest of the paragraph briefly outlines the methodology for the desired reform:

> For this purpose the rites are to be simplified [*simpliciores fiant*], due care being taken to preserve their substance [*substantia*]; elements which, with the passage of time, came to be duplicated, or were added with but little advantage, are now to be discarded; other elements which have suffered injury through accidents of history are now to be restored to the vigor which they had in the days of the holy Fathers, as may seem useful or necessary.

To what extent did Archbishop Bugnini respect the Council's wishes? How, and why, did he go well beyond them? That is what this book will seek to demonstrate. It is not a complete history of the postconciliar liturgical reform and of the crisis it precipitated; it is the story of a churchman who wished his tombstone to bear this epitaph: *Liturgiae cultor et amator, servì la Chiesa.*

---

6. *SC* 50.

ABBREVIATIONS

Bugnini, *Reform*: Annibale Bugnini. *The Reform of the Liturgy 1948–1975.* Trans. Matthew J. O'Connell. Collegeville, MN: Liturgical Press, 1990.

Bugnini, *Memorie*: Annibale Bugnini. *"Liturgiae Cultor et Amator, Servì la Chiesa."* *Memorie Autobiografiche.* Rome: Edizioni Liturgiche, 2012.

DOL: International Commission on English in the Liturgy, *Documents on the Liturgy, 1963–1979: Conciliar, Papal, and Curial Texts.* Collegeville, MN: Liturgical Press, 1982. References are to the *DOL* document numbers and, if more precision is warranted, to the sequential marginal numbers.

Lameri: Angelo Lameri. *La "Pontificia Commissio de Sacra Liturgia Praeparatoria Concilii Vaticani II": Documenti, Testi, Verbali.* Rome: Edizioni Liturgiche, 2013.

Marini: Piero Marini. *A Challenging Reform: Realizing the Vision of the Liturgical Renewal, 1963–1975.* Ed. Mark R. Francis, John R. Page, and Keith F. Pecklers. Collegeville, MN: Liturgical Press, 2007.

SC: Constitution on the Sacred Liturgy *Sacrosanctum Concilium* of the Second Vatican Council, 4 December 1963. *DOL* 1.1–131.

Translator's Note

YVES CHIRON's prolific output has made him an inescapable authority in modern Catholic Church history. His twenty-six books include discussions on the history of ecumenical councils (2011) and the apparitions at Medjugorje (2010), biographies of Padre Pio (1998) and Paul VI (1993), and most recently his biography of St. John XXIII in 2017. So far, only two of his works have been put into English: *Saint Pius X: Restorer of the Church* (2002) and *Pius IX: The Man and the Myth* (2005), both translated by Graham Harrison for Angelus Press.

The work we here present, *Mgr Bugnini (1912–1982): Réformateur de la liturgie* (Paris: Desclée de Brouwer, 2016), is of a piece with his work. It received positive reviews from such diverse readers as Fr G. de Tanoüarn (*Monde & Vie* 919 [3 February 2016]: 21: "un livre à méditer") and Nicolas Senèze (*La Croix* [18 February 2016]: "une biographie passionnante"). The importance of this biography's subject, Archbishop Annibale Bugnini, may be gauged from the full-page presentation that Fr Bernard Ardura, President of the Pontifical Committee for Historical Studies, devoted to him in *L'Osservatore Romano* (24 March 2016) on the occasion of the publication of this book.

Chiron earned his reputation as a serious historian with his commitment to the highest standards of historical criticism. These can be expressed as follows: the true historian relies on verifiable sources, not hearsay; he explores every avenue to get at relevant texts and documents; he compares witnesses; he "dares not lie," as Leo XIII recommended. Some readers will be disappointed at his unwillingness to go further than the strict interpretation of texts admits; others will regret the candor with which he states matters of fact.

Our translation follows the original French faithfully. Editorial notes are indicated by a dagger (†). We have used published English translations of French, Italian, and Latin sources whenever these were available, with minor changes when warranted. In all other cases, we have translated straight from the original language of Chiron's source. The notes follow the Continental norm of economy: a document is cited once in a given context without resort to multiple specific references. The interested reader with access to the sources will have no trouble tracking down the specific page numbers.

1

Formation and First Works

ANNIBALE BUGNINI was born in Civitella dei Pazzi, about twenty kilometers from Orvieto. It was one of the medieval popes' residences when they wished to avoid unrest in Rome. Today Civitella is a village overlooking Lake Corbora, lost amid the Umbrian hills.

Born on June 14, 1912 to Giobbe Bugnini and Maria Agnese *née* Ranieri, he was the fifth of seven children. His father was a simple sharecropper for several landowners around the village. He had had little education, as had his wife, but both were solidly pious. Every morning the mother gathered the children for the day's prayers according to Saint Pius X's *Little Catechism*, and in the evening for the Rosary and the traditional prayers before going to bed. The family was also very attached to the pilgrimage of Santa Maria de Scopulis, three hour's walk from Civitella. This little shrine was more commonly called La Pasquarella as it was usually visited during the Octave of Easter.

In the Bugnini family as in many Italian families of those days, faith and religious practice came naturally. Three of the children entered the religious life: Fidenzio would join the Servite Friars, Celestina the Daughters of Charity, Annibale the Vincentians.

Studies in Siena and Rome

Annibale first spent a year in Civitella's little elementary school; then, aged eight, he was brought to Siena by one of his aunts to continue his education there. While he was no brilliant pupil, he loved liturgical ceremonies very early on and would visit several churches to serve Mass or to sing in choir.

Religious feasts exerted a particular attraction on me. I didn't miss one. One way or another I sought to get into the sacristy and reach the altar. If I found a welcoming atmosphere there, I'd go back. I soon became friends with all the sacristans of Siena; as soon as they'd see me they'd put me into a cassock and send me to serve the liturgical functions.[1]

The year of his First Communion (1923), the religious sister who taught him his catechism, a Daughter of Charity named Germaine Corsini, asked him whether he had given the priesthood any thought.

"I unhesitatingly answered yes at the first inquiry, and have abided by that ever since," Archbishop Bugnini would later write. He added that this religious sister's advice through the years and the prayers she said for his intentions had been very important to him: "I owe my priesthood to her, after God."[2]

For over a year he had nearly weekly meetings with a Vincentian priest, Fr Testori, who also judged that the lad might have a solid vocation. The Apostolic School of the order was on the third floor of a large building on the Via Pompeo Magno, between the Vatican and the Tiber. This building also housed the novitiate of the Congregation of the Mission's Roman province.

Accordingly, at the end of the 1924 school year, on June 5, he left Siena to go to the Vincentians' Apostolic School in Rome,[3] the equivalent of what used to be called a minor seminary.

The Apostolic School pupils, though living in the house on the Via Pompeo Magno and attending services in its chapel, attended the classes of the Seminario Romano Minore, at the time located in Palazzo Santa Marta at the Vatican. And so, every day from October to June, the little Vincentian seminarians walked to the Vatican in two straight lines.

Annibale Bugnini spent four years at the Apostolic School (1924–1928). During the third year the young students expressing the

1. Bugnini, *Memorie*, 31–32.
2. Ibid., 33.
3. The members of the Congregation of the Mission (C.M.) are commonly called *Missionari di San Vincenzo* or *Vincenziani* in Italy. In English they are termed *Vincentians* while the French term *Lazaristes* is after the Saint-Lazare priory in Paris where the young congregation established itself in 1625.

intention of continuing their studies on to the priesthood received the cassock. For young Bugnini and his classmates, the "clothing ceremony" took place early in their third year, November 7, 1926.

He finished his secondary studies in June 1928, receiving the *licenza ginnasiale* from Umberto I State school. He quite naturally entered the Vincentian noviciate on October 5, 1928; it too was on the Via Pompeo Magno, as mentioned above. The Congregation of Missions' noviciate lasted two years. After the first year the novices undertook a first solemn engagement: the *proponimenti* ("resolutions"). The ceremony took place October 6, 1929.

First Teachers of the Liturgy

It was during the first two years of his noviciate that young Bugnini came into closer contact with liturgical studies.

The house on the Via Pompeo Magno also housed *Ephemerides Liturgicae*, a review founded in 1887 by the Vincentian Calcedonio Mancini. In 1928 the Vincentians wished to breath new life into this already old review and to give it a more historical orientation. They therefore called upon the services of Dom Cunibert Mohlberg of the Benedictine abbey of Maria Laach in Germany, one of the first centers of what came to be called "the Liturgical Movement." Dom Mohlberg had notably founded the review *Liturgie geschichtliche Quellen* in 1919. In Rome, besides his close collaboration with *Ephemerides Liturgicae*, he was liturgy professor at the Pontifical Institute of Christian Archeology and was taken on as *scrittore* at the Vatican Library.

Although at the time the young Bugnini was not in close relations with this specialist in liturgy, he read him and may well have met him on different occasions. Indeed in 1928–1930 the young Bugnini was asked to assist the review's secretariat during his free time at the noviciate. He sent the issues out when they were published, he entered subscriptions, and inevitably became familiar with what was then the oldest liturgy review in Italy. "It was the beginning of my liturgical vocation," he would later recount.[4]

4. Bugnini, *Memorie*, 36.

At about the same time and thanks to a noviciate classmate he discovered the great work of Dom Ildefonso Schuster (1880–1954). Schuster, who had entered the Abbey of Saint Paul Outside the Walls at a very young age, became its abbot in 1918.[5] From 1919 to 1932 he published a vast liturgical commentary in ten volumes, *Liber sacramentorum. Note storiche e liturgiche sul Messale Romano*.[6] Bugnini the novice discovered this vast work with passion: "I bought each volume as soon as it was published. I devoured and annotated them with a neophyte's enthusiasm. The 'Schuster' was my first master of liturgy."[7] Young Father Montini (the future Pope Paul VI) too had discovered Schuster's great work a few years before and used to attend the *ritiri minimi* ("short retreats") that this abbot ran at Saint Paul Outside the Walls.[8] This commonality between Bugnini and Montini would bring them closer when they were carrying out the liturgical reform together.

After two years' noviciate, a young Bugnini made his religious profession on October 6, 1930. These were simple vows; nevertheless, according to the congregation's constitutions, they constituted a definitive and solemn commitment to the Congregation of the Mission.

Two days later he left for Piacenza with four of his companions to begin his philosophy studies at the Collegio Alberoni as the first stage in his priestly formation. The director of the institution, Fr Alcide Giuseppe Marina (1886–1950),[9] a deeply cultured man, had undertaken the Italian translation of all fourteen volumes of Saint Vincent de Paul's writings as well as of the standard French-language biography of the founder of the Vincentians published by Fr

---

5. He was named archbishop of Milan in 1929 and created cardinal. He died in 1954 and was beatified by John Paul II in 1996.

6. English translation, in five volumes: *The Sacramentary (Liber Sacramentorum): Historical and Liturgical Notes on the Roman Missal*, trans. Arthur Levelis-Marke (London: Burns, Oates & Washbourne, 1924–30).

7. Bugnini, *Memorie*, 36.

8. Yves Chiron, *Paul VI. Le pape écartelé* 2nd ed. (Paris: Perrin, 2008), 43.

9. He would later be the Apostolic Delegate to Persia (Iran), then to Turkey, and lastly Apostolic Nuncio in Lebanon.

Pierre Coste. Fr Marina was also in charge of the *Annali della Missione* and endeavored to acquaint the scholastics with Vincentian spirituality and history during the lectures he gave them every week. It is at this time that a young Bugnini began his Vincentian studies which, beside the liturgy, were his other great interest and occasioned many of his published works to the end of his life.[10]

It was at the Collegio Alberoni that he met Silvio Oddi, who was two years older and was to pursue a successful career in papal diplomacy before being created cardinal and being named prefect of the Congregation for Clergy.

In autumn 1933 Bugnini returned to Rome to begin his theological studies at the Angelicum. He had rooms in his congregation's clerical student residence, which adjoined the church of San Silvestro al Quirinale. There he again met Silvio Oddi who, for his part, was undertaking his canon law studies.

These years at San Silvestro were punctuated with different ceremonies corresponding to as many steps towards the priestly estate: tonsure on December 24, 1933; minor orders on November 1, 1934 and April 13, 1935; subdiaconate on June 6, 1936; diaconate on the following July 5; lastly, priestly ordination on July 26, 1936. His ordination to the priesthood took place not at Rome, but at the San Vincenzo house in Siena, which had been dedicated the day before. Archbishop Marina, who ordained him to the priesthood, had been his first teacher in the Vincentian congregation, as we have seen. He had recently been consecrated bishop and was performing ordinations before leaving for Persia (now Iran), where he had just been appointed apostolic delegate.

Fr Bugnini's theological studies were crowned with a licentiate in theology. He received it on June 15, 1939, with a thesis titled *De Sacra Liturgia eiusque momento in Concilio Tridentino* ["On the sacred liturgy and its importance in the Tridentine Council"]. Archbishop

---

10. Bugnini was to manage the *Annali della Missione* from 1947 to 1957; in 1957 he would found the monthly *Vincentiana* and publish, in the *Enciclopedia Cattolica*, thirty-nine articles about Saint Vincent de Paul, the Congregation of the Mission, and its most illustrious members.

Bugnini himself would later admit that this licentiate thesis was no "masterpiece," but that the principal fruit of this scholarly work had been to familiarize him with the way in which a council operates. This knowledge was to prove quite useful to him when he was closely involved in the work of another council: Vatican II.

Meanwhile, in autumn 1938, young Fr Bugnini had been named director of the *Convitto Leoniano* that had just opened on Via Pompeo Magno. The *Convitto* housed young priests, Vincentian and others, studying in Rome. Pius XI had decided that young priests coming from all over Italy to study in Rome should no longer live independently but stay in one of the *convitti ecclesiastici* that the Congregation for Seminaries controlled.

Fr Bugnini enforced an austere regimen at the Leoniano: wake-up at half past five; meditation in common; Mass said by each of the priests at the *Convitto*; meals in common and in silence so as to listen to the lector; Rosary at the end of the day; a monthly day-long retreat; and five-day-long Spiritual Exercises at the beginning of the academic year.

Fr Bugnini ran this *Convitto* for five academic years, from 1938 to 1943. The war, and the experience he gained, led him to relax the rules somewhat since they were more suited to monks or religious than to young priest-students.

Running the *Convitto* did not keep Fr Bugnini from having other activities. During the 1939–1940 academic year, he attended a class in library and archive science at the Vatican Library and at the Vatican Secret Archives that earned him a diploma in June 1940. He then attended courses at the Pontifical Institute of Christian Archeology for three years. He attended classes in the different subjects offered there (history, archeology, epigraphy), but not in liturgy since Fr Mohlberg, who held the chair in liturgy, was in Switzerland and had been unable to return to Italy for the entire duration of the war. Nevertheless, Fr Bugnini obtained a licentiate from the Institute.

First Liturgical Experimentation

Looking at the history of the liturgy in the twentieth century one observes a double movement. On the one hand, there are the initiatives and the commitment of successive popes to renew the liturgy in an "organic development." It is often said that this movement got its start with the motu proprio *Tra le sollecitudini* (1903) in which Pius X took several initiatives in the field of sacred music to encourage "the active participation in the most holy mysteries and in the public and solemn prayer of the Church." The phrase "active participation of the faithful" was the watchword of the entire Liturgical Movement to come.

Pius X also initiated a vast attempt at reforming the breviary and liturgical calendar between 1911 and 1914.[11] The motu proprio *Abhinc Duos Annos* (1913) especially undertook to reform the liturgical calendar. Pius X, noting that the multiplying saints' feasts had largely encroached upon the Sunday and ferial cycle, wished to restore the Temporal (i.e., the liturgical cycle of the life of Christ) and reduce the Sanctoral (the cycle of saints' feasts).

Pius X did obtain significant results, but his two immediate successors (Benedict XV and Pius XI) were not to resume his liturgical work. The papacy did not take up and develop this liturgical task until Pius XII after World War II, as we shall see.

On the other hand and at the same time, a continuous and growing stream of studies, works, and initiatives flowed from Pius X's impetus; it would be called the Liturgical Movement.[12] Two works by Dom Lambert Beauduin of Mont César Benedictine monastery, *De Promovenda Sacra Liturgia* and *La vraie prière de l'Église* ("On promoting the sacred liturgy" and "The true prayer of the Church," both published in 1909) are traditionally considered to be the first beginnings of the Liturgical Movement.[†] It spread to dif-

---

11. See Honoré Vinck, *Pie X et les réformes liturgiques de 1911–1914. Psautier, bréviaire, calendrier, rubriques* (Münster: Aschendorff Verlag, 2014).

12. Dom Alcuin Reid's doctoral dissertation (and later monograph) has given a renewed historical perspective on this double movement: *The Organic Development of the Liturgy: The Principles of Liturgical Reform and Their Relation to the Twentieth-Century Liturgical Movement Prior to the Second Vatican Council*, 2nd ed. (San Francisco: Ignatius Press, 2005).

[†] Also of great significance was Beauduin's 1914 work *La piété de l'église: principes et faits*, which was subsequently translated into English by Dom Virgil Michel under the title *Liturgy, the Life of the Church*. This book reached a wide audience.—*Ed.*

ferent countries (Belgium, France, Germany, Italy[†]) and took a variety of forms: meetings, study days, reviews, "experiments."

Fr Bugnini gradually inserted himself into this Liturgical Movement from the early 1940s on. As part of his priestly ministry he conducted a first liturgical experiment of his own during the war and in the years that followed it.[13]

In 1943 his superiors asked him to assist the priests in charge of a Roman suburban neighborhood, the Borgata Gordiani, on Sundays and feast days. After that he and a young confrere were sent to another suburb, Borgata Prenestina. This neighborhood numbered about 2000 inhabitants—most of whom lived in shanties—and did not yet have parish of its own. There was only a chapel dedicated to Saint Agapetus, which had been built from leftover materials of the great Vatican Mission Exposition organized in Rome under Pius XI.

"This priestly presence once a week was truly a drop in the ocean. The spiritual and material needs were so numerous," Bugnini would say. The two priests were assisted by religious sisters and students who came to teach catechism, organize games and activities for the children, and visit families.

Fr Bugnini came every Sunday for three years to say Mass in this underprivileged neighborhood. This was where he experimented with a kind of dialogue Mass. This type of Mass had existed since the end of the 1920s, but usually involved either the faithful reciting the "responses and prayers" that were otherwise said by the server(s) or the simple recitation by the faithful of the *Gloria, Credo, Sanctus, Benedictus,* and *Agnus Dei.*[14]

Fr Bugnini would go much further to encourage the participation of the faithful at Mass: he had the assembly say aloud a sort of paraphrase of the text of the Mass. He described the liturgical innovation he introduced in the Borgata Prenestina as follows:

[†] In the United States of America, the Movement was pursued by and disseminated from St. John's Abbey in Collegeville, Minnesota.—*Ed.*

13. Bugnini, *Memorie,* 50–51, 62–63.

14. The Sacred Congregation of Rites issued a rescript (4375) in 1922 declaring the dialogue Low Mass licit. In 1935, the same Congregation answered a question from the Cardinal Archbishop of Genoa regarding the dialogue Mass in the following terms: "in accordance with decree n. 4375, it is for the Ordinary to decide whether,

I suddenly wondered: how could I have this people, with their elementary religious instruction, participate in the Mass? Above all, how could I make the children participate? I started out by painting big signboards with the easier responses for the people to say in Latin, and after a few tries I succeeded in having them said in unison. Then I did the same with signposts in Italian. This way, as the celebrant went ahead with the Mass in Latin on his end, a reader, generally one of the young catechists who came to help me on Sundays, made the people participate with Italian paraphrases based on the text. I knew that I had found the formula: the people willingly followed the Mass. The "inert and mute" assembly had been transformed into a living and prayerful assembly.

Soon, as we shall see, Fr Bugnini published a popular edition of this "paraphrased" Mass. It would reach a considerable circulation.

Director of *Ephemerides Liturgicae*

Just as he was beginning this liturgical initiative, harbinger of the vast reform whose architect he would be after the Council, Fr Bugnini also had control of a review that allowed him to broadcast his ideas for a liturgical reform.

Indeed, in 1945 he joined the directorship of the *Ephemerides Liturgicae* review where he stayed until 1963. This review, with which he had been familiar since 1928, was going through a difficult time as it had only ninety-six subscribers left. Fr Bugnini reorganized it and gave it a new orientation. The *giuridico-pratica* section (devoted to "rubrics"), which came out every month as a separate fascicle, was considerably cut back and now made up only part of the henceforth bimonthly review. The publication was essentially devoted to historical and theological studies on the one hand, and to "pastoral" considerations on the other. "It was necessary to listen

in individual cases, in view of all the circumstances, namely, the place, the people, the number of Masses which are being said at the same time, the proposed practice, though in itself praiseworthy, in fact causes disturbance rather than furthers devotion." T. Lincoln Bouscaren, *The Canon Law Digest: Officially Published Documents Affecting the Code of Canon Law, 1933–1942*, vol. 2 (Milwaukee: Bruce, 1956), 198–200.

to the voices that 'imperiously' privileged pastoral liturgy. I opened the doors to it."[15]

The review blossomed, thanks to other initiatives concerning the liturgy in which Fr Bugnini was involved. With him as director, the publication reached several thousands of subscribers.

15. Bugnini, *Memorie*, 48.

2

A Crucial Meeting

I N HIS MEMOIRS, Bugnini mentions a trip he took in the
"autumn of 1948" in France, Belgium, and Spain to visit different monasteries and make contact with circles of people
attached to liturgical renewal:

> I visited Solesmes, the recently minted "Centre de Pastorale
> Liturgique" which was holding one of its first Conferences at
> Thienlen [sic] near Chartres under the presidency of Fr Duployé. I
> also saw Mont César, where I met Abbot Capelle and Dom Botte. I
> visited Montserrat, Vitoria, Madrid.[1]

Fr Bugnini's recollections are a little muddled on this point. The
conference of the new CPL, in which the principal French-speaking
players of the Liturgical Movement of the time were to be found
(Beauduin, Leclercq, Duployé, Martimort), did not take place at
"Thienlin" but in a locality called Le Thieulin, a few kilometers
from Chartres; furthermore, it was not in the autumn of 1948, but
two years earlier, in September of 1946.

The difference between the two dates is not insignificant, for the
main initiatives that Bugnini was to undertake or be involved in in
1947—a vast survey on the liturgy and the foundation of the *Centro
di Azione Liturgica*—do not predate his journey in France and his
discovery of the CPL; rather, they followed them. It may therefore
be supposed that what Fr Bugnini saw and heard at Le Thieulin and
the encounters he had there were not without some influence on his
thought and undertakings. Fr Duployé provides the following witness: "A few days before the meeting at Le Thieulin I received a visit

1. Ibid.

from an Italian Vincentian who had asked to be invited to it, Fr Bugnini."[2] This, then, was his first contact with the French Liturgical Movement.

The Liturgical Movement in France after World War II was diverse. Experts in the liturgy (historians of the liturgy, sacramental theologians, specialists in sacred chant) were paying close attention to the experiments that were developing here and there, sometimes not without expressing critical judgments.

Historians have yet to establish an exhaustive account of the experiments, commonly termed *paraliturgies*, that were being conducted in different places in France at the time, as well as of all the "dialogue Masses" being tried out in different parishes. Here we shall only mention the "popular and missionary fêtes" that Fr Michonneau had been organizing since the beginning of the 1940s in the parish of Sacré Cœur de Colombes. Fr Martimort gave the following description of them at the time:

> There are spoken choral parts, plays, songs, acclamations, processions. Those who have attended these celebrations can give an account of the results obtained: a compact, authentically popular Mass forming a true community gathering, enlivened with an intense religious spirit, praying with all its soul. This is no ordinary sight; even the most biased observer cannot help feeling a deep emotion before it.[3]

Nevertheless, Fr Martimort pointed out the "limitations" of such liturgies and made diverse criticisms, notably regarding such assemblies' lack of "*ecclesial* character" and the risk of protestantization and of charismatic enthusiasm (this back in 1945!):

> The Church is not only the great missionary but also the hierarchically organized sacred meeting of those who praise the Lord. If one isn't careful one might gradually allow religious sentiment to find its way towards a sort of Protestantism in which the individu-

2. P. Duployé, *Les Origines du Centre de Pastorale Liturgique, 1943–1949* (Mulhouse: Salvator, 1968), 320, n. 7.

3. A.-G. Martimort, "Une expérience des paraliturgies: 'Fêtes missionnaires et populaires' du Sacré-Cœur de Colombes," *La Maison-Dieu* 3 (1945): 164.

alism of Christian life would be tempered only by charismatic meetings; the hierarchy would end up only seeming to be a purely administrative body.[4]

The CPL's Le Thieulin meeting took place September 16–22, 1946 under the presidency of Bishop Harscouët of Chartres, who had been friendly to the CPL from the outset. The explicit agenda was to reach seminaries, to attract their interest in the thoughts, work, and "experiments" of the Liturgical Movement.

Forty rectors and superiors of major seminaries answered the CPL's invitation. The "program of lessons" given there shows the broad array of subjects treated:[5]

- *Inventory of the Problems*, by Fr Perrot, rector of the Mission of France Seminary
- *The Liturgy as Training Ground for Asceticism*, by Dom Lambert Beauduin, OSB
- *The Artistic Formation of Clergy*, by Fr Regamey, OP
- *A Practical Liturgy Curriculum*, by Fr Martimort
- *A Problem of Ecclesiastical Humanism: The Current Secularisation of "Convivium,"* by Fr Duployé, OP
- *Towards a Pastoral Theology*, by Fr H.-M. Féret, OP
- *Formation in Sacred Chant*, by Dom Urbain Sérès, OSB
- *The Organization of Pastoral Activity and the Teaching of Ecclesiology*, by Fr Yves Congar, OP

Fr Duployé gave the following report on Fr Bugnini's participation at the Le Thieulin conference:

> The Father listened very attentively, without saying a word, for four days. As we were traveling back to Paris and the train was passing by the *Pièce d'eau des Suisses* ornamental basin in Versailles, he told me: "I admire what you are doing, but the greatest favor I can do you is never to say a word in Rome of what I have just been hearing."[6]

---

4. Ibid., 169.
5. Duployé, *Les Origines*, 315–20.
6. Ibid., 320, n. 7.

It is doubtless at Le Thieulin that Fr Bugnini met Msgr Chevrot, pastor of Saint Francis Xavier parish in Paris. Msgr Chevrot, who had been a participant in the work of the CPL from its inception and collaborated with *La Maison-Dieu*, would sometimes take bold initiatives in the liturgy. Did Msgr Chevrot perhaps invite the young Vincentian to pay him a visit in his Parisian parish? In any event, Fr Bugnini mentions as exemplary a kind of offertory rite that Msgr Chevrot had established in his parish:

> After the *Credo*, the altar boys come out of the sacristy with four or five baskets each; they go before the altar, genuflect, then go to the back of the church, giving out the baskets to every third pew. Once they have arrived at the back of the church, they go back up the aisle, receive the baskets in which the faithful have put their offerings, take their station on either side of the altar and hold the baskets in a gesture of offering until the Preface begins.[7]

Fr Bugnini was to remember this Parisian initiative when he had a new Offertory rite put together for the "New Mass" of 1969.

After Le Thieulin and Paris, Fr Bugnini stopped in Toulouse, where he met up with Fr Martimort who was teaching at the *Institut Catholique*.[8] The two men would remain in close relations and Bugnini would call on Martimort as consultor in the preparatory liturgy commission and later in the *Consilium*.

A Survey

"For years I'd been wondering whether it wouldn't be possible to rejuvenate the liturgy, 'ridding' it of the superstructures that had weighed it down over the centuries [*'sbaroccandola' dalle sovrastrutture che nel corso dei secoli l'avevano pesantemente aggravata*]."[9] The onset of his reflections on the subject dates to 1947. He would soon evoke as a general possibility "a streamlining of the liturgical appa-

---

7. Annibale Bugnini, "La communità e il rinnovamento liturgico attuale," *Annali della Missione* 69.6 (1962): 350.

8. Aimé-Georges Martimort, "L'histoire de la réforme liturgique à travers le témoignage de Mgr Bugnini," *La Maison-Dieu* 162 (1985): 127.

9. Bugnini, *Memorie*, 49.

ratus and a more realistic adaptation to the concrete needs of the clergy and faithful in the changing conditions of our day."[10]

Fr Bugnini came up with a project: launching a vast international survey on the liturgy through *Ephemerides Liturgicae*. The review's editorial board first wanted the Congregation of Rites to be consulted and to give its agreement. Fr Bugnini was received by that congregation's secretary, Msgr Carinci, and submitted his project to him. Not only did Msgr Carinci not oppose it, but he encouraged him. At the very same time Pius XII and the Congregation of Rites were planning to establish a pontifical commission for the general reform of the liturgy; we shall return to it. Msgr Carinci probably did not bring up this future commission to Fr Bugnini at that time (even though he was to belong to it when it was created). Still, he allowed the editor of *Ephemerides Liturgicae* to launch his initiative, while setting a few limits.

And so Fr Bugnini launched a survey in early 1948; it took the form of an extensive opinion poll. Under the aegis of *Ephemerides Liturgicae* he sent it to about a hundred ecclesiastics in various countries and continents. The idea, said Fr Bugnini, "was to have a fairly precise idea of the clergy's actual aspirations." As usual in any survey of this type, the addressees were carefully selected. Those who were questioned were

> university professors, seminary instructors, ecclesiastics active in ministry, charity directors, religious in various orders and congregations, missionaries, etc. Those particularly invited [to give their opinion] were persons who, by virtue of their ministry, such as preaching to the clergy, lecturers, directors of retreat houses, etc., are in frequent contact with many ecclesiastics.

No bishop had been polled. Yet if there was a category that is "in frequent contact with many ecclesiastics," it was they. But polling bishops and publishing their answers, even anonymously, would have lent a certain official character to the survey, which the Congregation for Rites doubtless opposed. The survey was therefore

---

10. Annibale Bugnini, "Per una riforma liturgica generale," *Ephemerides Liturgicae* 63.1 (1949): 166–84.

presented as being "entirely private and reserved." The survey was sent to its addressees with an assurance that their responses would not be published verbatim, and that no name would be mentioned.

Of the roughly one hundred persons polled, about forty sent in a response. These responses came in from diverse countries and varied in length. "Some simply stuck to the questionnaire that had been sent; others developed veritable dissertations," Bugnini would later say. The responses were not published unabridged; they were summarized, with quotations, and Bugnini added his own comments, as we shall see.

The *Centro di Azione Liturgica* (CAL)

At the same time, Fr Bugnini was involved in another initiative. The Liturgical Movement had been developing in Italy for many years. One of its principal figures was Dom Emmanuele Caronti (1882– 1966). Since 1914 he had been the first director of the *Rivista liturgica*. Then, once he was abbot of the San Giovanni Evangelista monastery in Parma, he had founded the *Bolletino liturgico* in 1923 to "popularize the Church's prayer in a pious and simple way accessible to all people of all classes." With the same purpose in mind he had also published two missals with translation and commentary that were widely published: *Il Messale festivo per i fedeli* from 1921 and a *Messale quotidiano per i fedeli* from 1929.

From the sixth to the tenth of October 1947,[11] the *Rivista liturgica* organized a few days of liturgical studies at the abbey of Parma. The point was to "organize on absolutely practical bases the Liturgical Action that needs to develop in Italy."[12] Only a small group of participants, twenty-two total, volunteered to meet, including Fr Bugnini. The keynote speech was given by Bishop Carlo Rossi of Biella. At the end of the conference, a "Voto" and a "Deliberazione" were adopted.

11. Here again Archbishop Bugnini has muddled the chronology, since he mentions the event in a few lines and places it in "autumn 1948" (*Memorie*, 60).

12. Agenda for the workshop quoted by Carlo Braga, "Il Centro di Azione Liturgica a servizio del Movimento liturgico," in *50 anni alla luce del Movimento liturgico* (Rome: Centro Liturgico Vincenziano–Edizioni Liturgiche, 1998), 50.

The "Wish" ("Voto") was expressed as follows:

The liturgical idea should spread ever more broadly, although it should also be known that the Liturgical Movement by no means intends to exclude the devotional patrimony of the Christian people. Rather, it wishes to make a positive contribution to an intense life of individual and collective piety; it intends to bring the faithful back to the Church from which they are growing ever distant.[13]

The "Deliberazione" was the decision to create a *Centro di Azione Liturgica* (CAL, Center of Liturgical Action). This initiative was in line with the centers of liturgical studies that had cropped up in the preceding years in Germany, in France (1943), and in Switzerland. Its very name ("Liturgical Action") asserted its determination not to rest content with historical and doctrinal studies, but to investigate concrete applications.

Fr Bugnini was among the founders of the CAL. Its first president was Bishop Carlo Rossi of Biella. In 1949 he yielded his position to Bishop Adriano Bernareggi of Bergamo. It was also from that year on that a *Settimana liturgica nazionale* ("National Liturgical Week") was organized. The first of these took place in Parma in September of 1949. The later ones took place yearly and brought together bishops, priests, and liturgy professors. Fr Bugnini gave lectures there quite regularly. One of his close associates, Fr Carlo Braga, was the CAL's secretary from 1959 on.

"Towards a General Liturgical Reform"

Also in 1949 Fr Bugnini published the results of the survey he had launched the year before. He did so in a long article dated March 1949, with a bold title: "Per una riforma liturgica generale" ("Towards a General Liturgical Reform").[14]

In truth this long article is not a systematic summary of the responses he had received. There are few direct quotations, and the authors' names are never cited; there are long comments by Fr Bug-

13. Ibid.
14. Bugnini, "Per una riforma liturgica generale," 166.

nini, however. Lastly, this article is less of an analysis of the responses received than a personal presentation that relies on the survey's contradictory results.

Fr Bugnini describes the liturgy of the time as "a mosaic, or if you prefer, an old building that has been erected little by little, at sundry times, with various materials and by diverse hands." He deems that "problems of a pastoral nature" require a liturgical reform that will "either be general or will end up leaving no one satisfied because it will have left things as they are with their deficiencies, their inconsistencies, and their difficulties."

Yet in this article Fr Bugnini is far from outlining the general plan of such a reform. He focuses on two aspects: liturgical feasts and the calendar on the one hand, and the breviary on the other. He defines a few principles, notably having the proper of the Temporal (the liturgical cycle based on the life of Christ) predominate over the Sanctoral (saints' feasts).

Regarding these areas, Fr Bugnini offered countless concrete proposals without making clear which were his own desiderata and which were conclusions drawn from the survey. He sometimes did so with the slightly abrupt tone that was often to be his trademark. Among his more salient proposals, Bugnini deemed necessary "a reduction of the Sanctoral ... which requires not only a reduction of the present calendar, but also fixed and prescriptive norms to prevent new Saints' days from piling up again."

A list of thirteen saints or groups of saints was already drawn up for elimination from the universal calendar, with no justification for any of them (Saint Martin for example), whereas the calendar was supposed to *abbinare* ("pair together") fourteen more Saints "because their life and work were alike or close to it," for example Saint Thomas Becket and Saint Stanislaus or Saint Peter Canisius and Saint Robert Bellarmine.

He also contemplated a reform of the structure of the breviary, "in which the prayers are to be distributed differently, for example in the morning and evening. It is a natural rhythm in human life that corresponds better to our present mode of life."

The point was to aim at "a reduction of the daily *pensum*" [task, burden].

At the end of his article, Bugnini admitted that he had "gleaned here and there in the abundant mass of the responses received." Doubtless because of lack of sufficient space he deliberately left aside considerations and suggestions bearing on other liturgical issues. Whatever the case may be, as it is and because of its boldness, this article was to attract attention. It was translated in an unabridged German version in *Bibel und Liturgie*, the review directed by Austrian Canon Pius Parsch in Klosterneuburg, and it received many reviews in several Italian and foreign journals.

3

The Reforms of Pius XII
(1945–1958)

A T THE TIME that Fr Bugnini was launching his first liturgical initiatives, Pius XII had already initiated an ambitious general reform of the liturgy. It manifested itself in decisions of varying import but remained largely unfinished.

The more noteworthy of his occasional decisions are: the mitigation of the Eucharistic fast in 1953; the authorization of evening Masses, first for prisoners unable to attend Mass in the morning because of prison rules in 1946, then for workers obliged to work on Sunday mornings in 1947; or again, the authorization granted to the bishop of Chartres on July 20, 1948, for his diocese to have the Epistle and the Gospel read out in French after their being chanted in Latin.[1] This last permission was soon granted to other French dioceses, and to all of France in 1956.

The Bea Psalter

Revising the Latin translation of the psalms was among the projects closest to Pius XII's heart. He thought, as did a number of theologians, exegetes, and scholars of the day, that the then-current translation used in the Church—the Vulgate—contained too many deficiencies. He was soon to say:

> In our day, however, these obscurities and inaccuracies are becoming ever more glaring. For recent times have witnessed remarkable progress in the mastery of oriental languages, particularly Hebrew,

---

1. *La Voix de Notre-Dame de Chartres* 32 (20 November 1948): 133.

and in the art of translation. Scholarly research into the laws of
meter and rhythm governing oriental poetry has advanced apace.
The rules for what is called textual criticism are now seen in
clearer light.[2]

What he wanted was a new translation "to follow the original
texts, follow them exactly, faithfully." He therefore had a new translation of the psalter made in the very first years of his pontificate.
He did not involve the Biblical Commission; rather, he entrusted
the task to Fr Augustine Bea, the German Jesuit president of the
Pontifical Biblical Institute. The latter worked at it from 1941 to 1944
with the assistance of five Institute professors. The result, far from
being a revision of existing versions, was a new translation of the
Hebrew text into classical Latin. This new version, the *Liber Psalmo-
rum*, was published in 1945.

There was much criticism of this new Latin translation. Cardinal
Tisserant, president of the Biblical Commission, said nothing in
public but reproved its "German pedantry" (four of the six transla-
tors were German Jesuits).[3] Several theological and liturgical
reviews published critical articles. Most noteworthy is the long editorial series put out by *La Maison-Dieu*, the publishing arm of the
Centre de Pastoral Liturgique, under the title "Débat sur le nouveau
psautier" ("A Debate on the New Psalter").[4] While hailing the significance of this bold initiative ("No one doubts that the appearance of
a new psalter, after sixteen centuries of Saint Jerome's psalter being
in use, constitutes an event"), the journal, after several critical studies by various Benedictines and Dominicans, judged that the new
psalter was "too radically changed" and asked that it should not be
"imposed on us *as is*." It was a stern judgment: the new translation's
Latin was too classical, excessively closer to "the language of Cicero
and Horace" than to the Latin of the Church. "If greater intelligibil-

---

2. Motu proprio *In Cotidianis Precibus*, 24 March 1945, *AAS* 37 (1945): 65, in the
Enchiridion biblicum: documenti della chiesa sulla sacra Scrittura (Bologna: Edizioni
Dehoniane, 1994), n. 572; Eng. trans. *Orate Fratres* 19 (17 June 1945): 337–40.

3. In a conversation with Yves Congar reported in the latter's *Journal d'un théo-
logien*, *1946–1956* (Paris: Cerf, 2000), 77.

4. *La Maison-Dieu* 5 (1946): 60–106.

ity of prayer for generations of priests who are less and less imbued with a classical culture is what is sought in a new version of the psalter, one turns his back on the goal in giving them a prayer composed in a special language with a refined vocabulary."

These criticisms hurt Pius XII; he considered them to be a "personal attack," some said.[5] Fr Bea wrote a book attempting to explain the work of the commission he had directed and to justify the result.[6]

In his motu proprio *In Cotidianis Precibus* of March 24, 1945, Pius XII had offered this new translation of the psalter (without imposing it on the whole Church) "to all who have the obligation to recite the canonical Hours daily," and he gave authorization for it to be included in and adapted to the Roman breviary.[7]

This revised translation, more usually called the "Bea Psalter," was adopted by only a few religious and monastic communities. On the other hand, it was included in the new editions of the breviary to be published. But common opinion insisted that the Bea Psalter *adauget latinitatem, minuit pietatem* ("increases Latinity and diminishes piety"). It did not manage to impose itself; during the revision of the breviary undertaken during the pontificate of John XXIII, this ill-suited translation was abandoned.

This first liturgical reform of Pius XII's can be said to have been a failure. Yet he was not discouraged. On May 10, 1946, Cardinal Salotti, prefect of the Congregation of Rites, presented to the pope the idea of instituting a commission for the general reform of the liturgy.[8] The idea was all the more congenial to Pius XII in that it cor-

---

5. The expression is that used by Cardinal Tisserant and Msgr Montini, substitute at the Secretariate of State, within a few days of each other in conversations with Fr Congar: Congar, *Journal*, 76, 108.

6. Augustin Bea, *Die neue lateinische Psalmenübersetzung, ihr Werden und ihr Geist* (Freiburg: Herder, 1949).

7. *Enchiridion biblicum*, n. 575.

8. Besides Giampietro, *The Development of the Liturgical Reform* (see p. 11, n. 4 above), see the (incomplete) edition by Carlo Braga, *La riforma liturgica di Pio XII. Documenti*, vol. 1, *La "Memoria sulla riforma liturgica"* (Rome: Centro Liturgico Vincenziano Edizioni Liturgiche, 2003).

responded to his own plans. On July 27, 1946, Msgr Carici, secretary at the same Congregation, brought up the same idea to the pope.

In 1947, Pius XII published a lengthy encyclical on the liturgy, *Mediator Dei et Hominum*. In it, he defined the liturgy as the "external" worship rendered unto God, while asserting that "the chief element of divine worship must be interior. For we must always live in Christ and give ourselves to Him completely, so that in Him, with Him, and through Him the heavenly Father may be duly glorified."[9]

Without going into the details of this encyclical, it is worth mentioning that the pope underscores that the liturgy, "its organization, regulation, and details, cannot but be subject to Church authority." While deploring arbitrary initiatives such as an exaggerated attachment to "ancient rites and ceremonies," the pope granted that it was legitimate to "introduce . . . new rites" and to "modify" current rites, but he drew attention to the fact that this right belongs to "the Sovereign Pontiff alone."

Pius XII insisted that distinctions be maintained on several points. The "participation of the faithful," to which the pope devoted a whole section of his encyclical, is not to be mistaken for a truly "priestly power" granted to the faithful. Pius XII was also fighting against false notions of "concelebration," of communion, and of so-called private Masses. He encouraged Eucharistic worship ("exercises of piety [that] have brought a wonderful increase in faith and supernatural life to the Church militant") and the fourth and last section of the encyclical was devoted to quite concrete "pastoral directives."

The encyclical was "justifiably defined as the *magna charta* of the healthy Liturgical Movement, to which it gave a new impetus by indicating its limits and determining its orientations."[10]

---

9. Pius XII, Encyclical *Mediator Dei* of 20 November 1947 (Boston: St. Paul Editions, 1990), n. 24.

10. Ferdinando Antonelli, "L'istruzione della S. Congregazione dei Riti sulla Musica sacra e la sacra Liturgia," *L'Osservatore Romano,* 2 October 1958; English trans. in *Worship* 32.10 (1958): 626–37.

The *Commissio Piana*

On May 28, 1948, Pius XII set up a Pontifical Commission for the Reform of the Liturgy that was eventually to be termed *Commissio Piana*. It was created within the Congregation of Rites, with Cardinal Micara, the new prefect of the same Congregation, as its president. Its creation was not made public; for a long time it worked in secrecy. Only when the first of the reforms it had prepared was promulgated was its existence revealed to the greater number, including most liturgists. It numbered few members and, unlike the commissions that later pontificates were to establish, it relied on few liturgy experts.

With Cardinal Micara as president, the Pontifical Commission for the Reform of the Liturgy originally numbered only six members: Archbishop Alfonso Carinci, undersecretary of the Congregation of Rites; Fr Ferdinando Antonelli, OFM, relator general of the historical section of the Congregation of Rites; Fr Josef Löw, CSSR, vice-relator general of the same historical section; Fr Anselmo Albareda, OSB, prefect of the Vatican Library; Fr Augustin Bea, SJ, rector of the Pontifical Biblical Institute; and Fr Bugnini who, in his capacity as director of *Ephemerides Liturgicae*, was named secretary of this commission.

Later on Bugnini would exercise the same function of secretary in the conciliar preparatory commission on the liturgy as well as in the postconciliar *Consilium* for liturgical reform. Yet whereas he played a decisive role in the preparatory commission and in the *Consilium*, he did not have a leading role on the *Commissio Piana*. He was an invaluable worker[11] and rarely intervened in the discussions. He learned and observed much, probably became aware of certain problems, but never exerted a decisive influence.

Without making a detailed list of the work of this Commission for the Reform of the Liturgy, which operated up until the Second Vatican Council, one can establish a quick summary of its results and of the reforms it passed successfully.

---

11. For example, he drew up the analytic and general indices of the *Memoria sulla Riforma liturgica* edited by Antonelli and Löw.

The commission held eighty-two meetings, from June 22, 1948 to July 8, 1960. At the very first meeting, it was established that the endeavor was to be a "general reform of the liturgy," although there existed no general plan.

On December 30, 1948 the Tipografia Poliglotta Vaticana printed a 343-page-thick volume titled *Memoria sulla Riforma liturgica* ("Report on the Liturgical Reform").[12] This study, which was not meant to be made public (it came to be known only in 1962), was due to the collaborative work of Fr Antonelli and Fr Löw. Its first chapter presented the "need for a liturgical reform." The second chapter defined the "fundamental principles" to guide it: "to strike a balance between the opposite demands of the conservative tendency and of the innovating tendency" and to make the Temporal and ferial cycles "predominate" over the Sanctoral. The third chapter, which took up the largest section of the volume, outlined an "Organic Program" in nine points: a revision of the gradation of feasts, of the calendar, of the breviary, of the Mass, of the Martyrology, of the *Libri cantus*, of the Roman Ritual, of the Ceremonial of Bishops, of the Roman Pontifical, and of the *Codex iuris liturgici*.

The first two points alone were elaborated at length, while the others were just given somewhat brief orientations. For example, in the case of the Mass it was specified that the reforms to be envisaged "would not deal so much with the Missal as with the Mass as celebrated in its external form and in the manners of attending it" (i.e., the use of modern languages in the liturgy, the forms and methods of participation in the Mass).

The ambitious program outlined in this *Memoria* could not be completed. There were only partial, though striking, reforms:

• Decree of February 9, 1951 restoring the Paschal Vigil, with the blessing of the new fire and of the paschal candle, the blessing of the baptismal font, and the renewal of baptismal promises.

---

12. A facsimile reproduction is in Braga, *La Riforma*, 3–382. [Only 300 copies of the *Memoria* were printed, for private circulation *sub secreto* among those whom the Sacred Congregation of Rites wished to consult. See Reid, *Organic Development,* 151.—Ed.]

- Decree of March 23, 1955 for the simplification and reduction of the rubrics for Mass and Vespers.
- Decree of November 16, 1955 reforming the *Ordo* of Holy Week, notably restoring the ceremonies of Holy Thursday, Good Friday, and Holy Saturday "to [their] original evening time."[13]

To these decrees of the Congregation of Rites may be added the Apostolic Constitution *Christus Dominus* of January 6, 1953,[14] which relaxed the rules of the Eucharistic fast (limiting the fast to one hour before communion "by reason of some serious inconvenience"[†]), and broadened the possibility of celebrating Mass in the evening, whereas the Code of Canon Law specified (can. 821): "The beginning of the celebration of Mass shall not occur earlier than one hour before first light or later than one hour after noon."

Pius XII granted to the bishops, "should circumstances render this necessary," the right to set the time of Mass after "four o'clock in the afternoon."

The 1958 Instruction

The *Instruction on Sacred Music and the Sacred Liturgy* published by the Congregation of Rites in 1958 is yet another fruit of the *Commissio Piana*. It is dated September 3, 1958, a month before Pius XII passed away. It is weighty not only in its length but also in its twofold aim.

---

13. Giampietro, *Development*, 65.

14. *AAS* 45 (1953): 15–24; English version in John C. Ford, *The New Eucharistic Legislation. A Commentary on "Christus Dominus"* (New York, P.J. Kennedy and Sons, 1953), 3–43.

† This is not quite accurate. In the Apostolic Constitution *Christus Dominus* of 1953, Pius XII, though upholding the centuries-old fast from midnight onwards, ruled (among other things) that the fast was not broken by water, medicine for the sick, water-only ablutions in successive Masses, and a beverage taken by a priest with onerous pastoral work or after a long journey. For evening Masses, a fast from food for three hours and from non-alcoholic beverages for one hour was permitted. In the motu proprio *Sacram Communionem* of 1957, these concessions were further developed.—*Ed.*

On the one hand, it is the concrete application of the teachings that Pius XII had issued in his great encyclicals on the liturgy (*Mediator Dei*, 1947) and on sacred music (*Musicae Sacrae Disciplina*, 1955). On the other hand, it takes into account certain demands and aspirations of the Liturgical Movement, while intending to set limits to it. Fr Antonelli, relator general at the Congregation of Rites, expressed it clearly:

> The Instruction, be it said at once, is not meant as a floodgate for the Liturgical Movement. Rather, it is meant as a dike to protect it, in order that the movement, remaining within the riverbed of the great principles repeatedly inculcated by the Holy See, may truly carry the living waters of the Savior to all the faithful through an ever more active and conscious participation in the liturgical life of the Church.[15]

This Instruction therefore reveals, in what it authorizes and in the limits it establishes, the advances and the expectations of the Liturgical Movement, as well as what the center of authority (the pope and the Congregation of Rites) granted and what it deemed to be unacceptable.

The document is organized in three broad sections and 118 points.[16] Without detailing this Instruction in all of its specifics, one may note three salient points: the participation of the faithful; concelebration; sacred chant and music.

The participation of the faithful was given a precise definition with several distinct levels (n. 22):

> This participation must above all be *internal*, with that pious attention of mind and affection of heart ... [that is] more complete if *external* participation is added to internal attention, that is, participation shown by external actions, such as bodily posture (kneeling, standing, sitting), or by ritual gestures, and especially by the responses, prayers, and song.... Finally, complete active

15. Ferdinando Antonelli, "L'istruzione," *L'Osservatore Romano*, 2 October 1958; English translation in *Worship* 32 (1958): 628.

16. Sacred Congregation of Rites, *Instructio de Musica sacra et sacra liturgia* AAS 25 (1958): 630–63; trans. J.B. O'Connell (Westminster, MD: The Newman Press, 1959).

participation is achieved when a *sacramental* participation [i.e., communion] is added.

In solemn Masses (n. 25), the "first degree" of the active participation of the faithful consists in sung "liturgical responses": *Amen*; *Et cum spiritu tuo*; etc. The "second degree" is achieved once all the faithful also sing the parts of the Ordinary of the Mass: *Kyrie*; *Gloria*; *Credo*; *Sanctus-Benedictus*; *Agnus Dei*. Lastly, the "third degree" is attained when all in attendance are "so skilled in Gregorian chant that they are capable of singing also the parts of the Proper of the Mass."

Many at the time judged the question of liturgical language to be a determining factor for a better participation of the faithful. The Instruction recalled that for "liturgical functions the language is Latin," but that "in exercises of piety any language suitable for the faithful may be used" (n. 13). More specifically (n. 14):

> In high Masses Latin alone is to be used not only by the celebrant and ministers, but also by the choir or the faithful.... In *low* Masses the priest-celebrant, his server, and the faithful who *directly* take part in the liturgical action with the celebrating priest, namely, who say aloud those parts of the Mass that concern them, must use only Latin.
>
> If, however, in addition to this *direct* liturgical participation, the faithful wish to add some prayers or popular chants, according to local custom, this they may do also in the vernacular.

It is also recalled that "the saying aloud, with the celebrating priest, in Latin or in a word-for-word translation, of the parts of the *Proper*, *Ordinary*, or *Canon of the Mass* . . . by all the faithful or by a commentator, is strictly forbidden" (n. 14).

In keeping with an already widespread usage following concessions Rome had granted to certain countries, the Instruction specified that at "low Masses on Sundays and feast days . . . it is desirable that for the benefit of the faithful the Gospel, and also the Epistle, should be enunciated by a reader in the vernacular" (n. 14).

The 1958 Instruction also distinguished different specific types of Mass: conventual (which several priests attend but only one celebrates); concelebrated; and synchronized. It repeated the teachings of Pius XII (1954 and 1956) and of the Holy Office (1957) on concelebration, without extending its applicability. It also forbade so-called "synchronized" Masses, in which "two or several priests, at one or several altars, so celebrate Mass simultaneously that all the actions are done, all the words spoken, at one and the same moment. . . ."

A large portion of the Instruction was devoted to sacred music and chant. It distinguished sacred music, which may be used in liturgical actions (Mass, etc.), and religious music, which is apt to "arouse religious feelings in its hearers," but which "may not be admitted into liturgical functions" and hence cannot be performed in churches (n. 54). As for Gregorian chant, defined as "the chief and special sacred chant of the Roman Church" (n. 16), "not only may it be used in all liturgical functions but . . . it is to be preferred to other kinds of sacred music."

The Instruction made allowances for the particular situation of mission countries and territories far removed from Western culture (n. 112). Bearing in mind the traditional distinction between "liturgical actions" and "exercises of piety," it prescribed that "the missionaries should aim at adapting their native music to sacred use, *servatis servandis*; let them take pains so to arrange exercises of piety that the native Christians may be able to express their religions sentiments in their own language and in melodies suited to their own people."

Without using the term "inculturation," which was not yet current, the Instruction recommended that "where the family and social life of these peoples is imbued with a deep sense of religion, missionaries must take great care not only not to destroy this religious sense, but—having weeded out any superstition—rather to christianize it."

Reform of the Breviary

The *Commissio Piana* had also prepared a reform of the breviary. The Divine Office, whose origins are quite ancient, had undergone a vast reorganization after the Council of Trent with the *Breviarium Romanum* promulgated in 1568. It remained in use until the early twentieth century. Pius X then created a Commission for the Reform of the Breviary. The point was to restore the continuous recitation of the psalter over the course of a single week (as in the Benedictine tradition) and to reestablish the primacy of the Temporal over the Sanctoral, i.e., of the ferias of the liturgical cycle over saints' days.

The new breviary was promulgated in 1911. Among its novelties besides those just mentioned was the reduction of the number of psalms read or sung at Matins (down from twelve to nine). Then, in the following decades, bilingual editions of the breviary were developed in several countries to take into account the decline of Latin, including among the clergy.

Pius XII had included the reform of the breviary among the tasks of the *Commissio Piana*. In 1955, Cardinal Gaetano Cicognani, prefect of the Congregation of Rites, had proposed a survey of the bishops in this regard. It was decided to send it only to metropolitan archbishops and to archbishops and bishops directly subject to the Holy See. From 1956 to 1957, the *Commissio Piana* received 341 responses (out of 400 letters sent out). A summary of the results and excerpts of the responses were printed in a single volume not intended for publication.[17]

Without giving an exhaustive analysis of this summary and of the responses received, we shall merely note that the most frequent requests were to simplify the hymns (23.3%), to use the vernacular for the recitation of the breviary (17.9%), and to establish a single Nocturn (17.3%).

The preparatory commission for the Council was to rely on this survey to make its proposals for the reform of the breviary. Fr Bugnini would say: "The fourteen years I spent working in the Commission for the Reform of the Liturgy made me particularly sensitive to the *ratio pastoralis*, and gave me a certain flexibility of movement between the old and the new."[18]

17. *Memoria sulla Riforma liturgica*, Suppl. IV, *Consultazione dell' episcopate intorno alla riforma del Breviario romano (1956–1957). Risultati e deduzioni* (Rome: Tipografia Poliglotta Vaticana, 1957); facsimile reproduction in Braga, *La Riforma*, 649–785.

18. A. Bugnini, "La Communità e il rinnovamento liturgico attuale," *Annali della Missione* 69.6 (1962): 346.

4

From "Paraphrased Mass" to Liturgical Weeks

F R Bugnini's participation in the workings of the *Commissio Piana* was only one aspect of his activity during all those years.

He taught in several pontifical universities and religious institutions. From 1949 on, he was liturgy professor at the Pontifical University Urbaniana, which depended on the Congregation for the Propagation of the Faith in charge of missions. He taught there until 1964 and formed many priests from different continents. When, in 1967, he accompanied Paul VI to Kampala, Uganda, as delegate to pontifical ceremonies, he said that during the main celebration he saw himself "surrounded by a great number of African bishops" who remembered their professor and his lectures in which he "taught everything that came later with the Council."[1]

From 1955, he also taught at the Pontifical Institute of Sacred Music on the invitation of Msgr Higinio Anglés, a Spanish musicologist who had been the Institute's president since 1947 and had spearheaded a critical edition of the Gradual in collaboration with the abbey of Saint-Pierre de Solesmes. Fr Bugnini, however, had no particular qualifications in musicology and was not associated with the project. Later on, in the conciliar preparatory commission on the liturgy, Msgr Anglés would come into conflict with Fr Bugnini over sacred music.

From 1957, Fr Bugnini was also professor of pastoral liturgy at the Lateran Pontifical University. An Institute of pastoral theology had

1. Bugnini, *Memorie*, 57.

just been created within the Lateran under the presidency of Fr Raimundo Spiazzi. The very name of this new institution indicated its aims and the twenty lectures on pastoral liturgy that Fr Bugnini gave there every year were geared not to the history of the liturgy or to a doctrinal analysis, but to its practical applications and finality. Fr Bugnini taught this course until 1962, at which time he was "driven out" of the Lateran, to use his own term.

At the time, Fr Bugnini summarized what he thought were the fundamental elements of pastoral liturgy:

1. Active and conscious participation of all the faithful in the liturgy.
2. Livelier sense of community, i.e., a sense of the "holy assembly."
3. Emphatic return to biblical, patristic, and liturgical sources.
4. Use of action in the liturgy.
5. Wide use of popular religious song.[2]

These are the principles that Fr Bugnini would implement once he directed the liturgical reform after the Council.

Self-Publisher

The "paraphrased" Mass with which Fr Bugnini had experimented at Borgata Prenestina, as we have seen, seemed to him applicable to many other parishes.

On May 26, 1949, Pope Pius XII promulgated a papal Bull, *Iubilaeum Maximum*, to announce the Holy Year extending from Christmas 1949 to Christmas 1950. Millions of the faithful were to come to Rome from many countries. Thousands of Masses were to be celebrated outside of the traditional setting of Roman parishes. This seemed to Fr Bugnini the ideal moment to make known and to disseminate "his" "paraphrased" Mass.

The Central Committee for the Holy Year in charge of coordinating and facilitating the pilgrimages and of organizing the ceremonies published a *Pilgrim's Book* containing a guide to Rome, the four Jubilee Basilicas, songs, and prayers. This pilgrim's handbook was

---

2. Bugnini, "La communità," 349.

published in several languages and distributed in the hundreds of thousands of copies. Fr Bugnini had the idea of inserting the text of his "paraphrased Mass" into it, as he thought that priests coming from the world over with pilgrim groups might use it.

He submitted the text to the president of the Central Committee for the Holy Year, Msgr Ercole, who had Fr Bugnini's project examined by a liturgical authority, Dom Emanuele Caronti, author of missals with translation and commentary, as we have seen. His exact judgment regarding this "paraphrased Mass" project remains unknown, but it cannot have been positive: Msgr Ercole gave Bugnini his draft back, as "it was not judged opportune to publish it under the authority of the Committee."[3]

Fr Bugnini then turned to his congregation. His superiors refused to have his work published, "saying that it would be absolutely futile." Nevertheless, Fr Bugnini persisted in his project and decided to publish his "paraphrased Mass" at his own expense. The *Ephemerides Liturgicae* printer agreed to print an initial run of 10,000 copies, on credit. This small, 36-page brochure fit easily into a pocket. It sold at a very low price, far less than a missal, as a way to spur sales.

Fr Bugnini had advertisements published in journals run by the Congregation of the Mission. About fifty copies were sent to pastors of parishes "in the most forsaken and abandoned areas of central and southern Italy." A number of parishes throughout Italy sent in orders. The brochure was prodigiously successful.

La Nostra Messa

The first edition of the "paraphrased Mass" came out in late 1949. It was a small brochure about thirty pages long, with the telling title *La Nostra Messa* ["Our Mass"]. To edit and publish this booklet Fr Bugnini had the help of a young theology student in the Congregation of the Mission, Carlo Braga, who would remain a close collaborator throughout his career.

3. Bugnini, *Memorie*, 51.

La Nostra Messa presented itself as a "little handbook for communal participation at Holy Mass."[4] This was not a bilingual missal
such as those that existed in many other countries. It was rather a
little booklet allowing the faithful not only to follow the Mass as celebrated by the priest, but also to take an active part in it.

Following the formula that had been tried out in Borgata Prenestina, the basic principle of this "dialogue Mass" was the role of a *let-
tore* ("reader") whose continuous presentation during the Mass was
intended to assist the faithful and direct their participation while
the priest was at the altar. The Reader started his commentary out
loud as soon as the priest arrived at the altar and hardly stopped
until the end of the Mass. He would provide a commentary on
every one of the celebrant's gestures and read out an Italian translation of the words the priest said in Latin.

The other one of this missal's bold novelties was to give the Italian text next to the Latin. This Italian text was there not only for
comprehension (as in other bilingual missals of that era) but also so
that the faithful may say it aloud or sing it in Italian while the priest
spoke or sang it in Latin. For the most part the Reader alternated
songs and responses with the faithful in Italian.

In other sections yet, particularly the Offertory, rather than giving the translation of the prayers the priest was saying, the Mass
that Fr Bugnini developed had the Reader give a commentary on
the ritual acts and had the faithful say out loud, in Italian, prayers to
go along with all of the celebrant's gestures. For example, at the
washing of hands, rather than providing a translation of the psalm
verses the priest was saying (*Lavabo inter innocentes...*), the booklet
had the Reader explain the gesture ("The Priest washes his fingers
because he will soon touch the Body of Christ with them"), and
then had the faithful say a prayer out loud in Italian: "Purify, O
Lord, the hands of your minister and purify our hearts."

4. *La Nostra Messa* had a considerable circulation in Italy down to the early
1960s, yet no copy of this brochure is to be found in French libraries, not even in
the Vincentian archives (on Rue de Sèvres in Paris), even though they preserve a
great number of Bugnini's monographs and articles. Copies of this liturgical booklet are only to be found in Italian religious libraries. References here are to *La Nostra Messa* 11th ed. (Rome: Edizioni Liturgiche, 1959).

The consecration was the only time when the Reader paused his commentary and the faithful remained silent. The reader invited them to pray in silence: "We are at the most solemn moment of the Holy Mass. In a few instants, the sacrifice of the Cross will be renewed on the altar in a mystical, yet real, way. Let us recollect ourselves in adoration of the mystery of faith." Yet the booklet, rather than giving the text of the Roman Canon with an Italian translation, gave a few short prayers for the layman to say "quietly."

This "dialogue Mass" was therefore also a Mass "led" by a Reader who was a sort of intermediary between the priest and the faithful. The Reader, according to the booklet, could be "a priest, a member of the clergy, a member of Catholic Action, or a woman" (in the last case, the female reader intervened from her pew among the faithful, but "in such a way that her voice be audible"). *La Nostra Messa* was very bold on several points and did not respect all of the norms then in force.

Although Fr Bugnini is not mentioned by name, the following report that Bishop Charrière of Lausanne, Geneva, and Fribourg sent to the *Commissio Piana* in 1956 doubtless amounts to a critical reaction to Bugnini's "dialogue" and "directed" Mass:

> A movement has arisen in the Church to broaden the use of missals that have the Latin text on one page and the modern language text on the other. This movement has produced excellent results. Let us allow it to continue and gain strength, and let us not follow those who now would like us no longer to use missals but rather to listen to a sort of Coryphaeus [leader of the choir in ancient Greek drama] whose task it would be to speak throughout the Mass and, in a word, to set up a screen between the priest and the faithful. In all things, one must strike a balance.[5]

This liturgical booklet soon reached a high circulation. The first printing ran out within a few months, which allowed Fr Bugnini to pay the printer and to have a second printing made. Soon the Ediz-

---

5. Report written by Bishop Charrière and dated December 14, 1956, in *Memoria sulla Riforma liturgica*, suppl. 4 (1957), 100 (in C. Braga, *La Riforma liturgica*, 746).

ioni Liturgiche, official publisher of the Congregation of the Mission, took over the printing costs and were in charge of publishing *La Nostra Messa*, which only increased its circulation. The fifth edition came out in 1953, amounting to a total circulation of 100,000 copies; in 1962, the twelfth and last edition came out for a total of 1,500,000 copies sold. This brochure also underwent an English edition, published in Manila for the Philippines in 1960, and a Hindi edition published in Goa for India in 1961.

Liturgical Congresses

The 1950s, during which the various reforms undertaken by Pius XII took place, were also a decade of liturgical congresses and week-long seminars. There is no need to go into each one in detail, but it is worthwhile to point out the more relevant ones and those in which Fr Bugnini and the CAL were involved.

The "active participation of the faithful" in the liturgy was one of this period's recurring themes well before it became the watchword of the reform that Vatican II envisaged. In September 1953, Cardinal Lercaro, Archbishop of Bologna, made it the theme of his keynote address at the International Meeting for Liturgical Studies at Lugano, Italy: "Active participation, the fundamental principle of Pius X's pastoral and liturgical reform." Two years later, he published a diocesan liturgical directory for Bologna with this meaningful title: *A messa, figlioli! Direttorio liturgico per la partecipazione attiva dei fideli alla santa messa letta* ("To Mass, My Children! Liturgical Directory for the Active Participation of the Faithful at Low Mass"). This directory circulated widely.[6]

More meaningful yet was the seventeenth week-long liturgical conference in North America held in London, Canada, August 20–23, 1956. It brought together several hundreds of participants from the United States and English-speaking Canada under the presidency of Archbishop O'Hara of Kansas City. At the end of the Congress, the American Liturgical Commission drew up a list of

---

6. A first edition in 1955, a second in 1956, and a third in 1960.

"resolutions," with the desire to see Pius XII's "liturgical reform continue."[7] This American congress's twenty resolutions largely overlap those proposed by others in Europe. They bear on the Mass and the breviary, notably asking for "the practice ... of Mass facing the people to be encouraged" (n. 3); for "the Mass of the Catechumens in the vulgar language to be authorized" (n. 7); for a greater share of scriptural texts to be read in the Mass by establishing "a three or four-year cycle of readings" (n. 8); "for the prologue of the Gospel according to Saint John, which is currently said after the *Ite Missa est*, to be the priest's private and optional prayer" (n. 17); for the practice of concelebration to be broadened to include "synods, retreats, and other large gatherings of clergy" at the discretion of the local bishop (n. 18); for priests "who are involved in active ministry to be allowed to recite the breviary in their own language" (n. 20). Many of these resolutions were to be taken up by the conciliar preparatory commission on the liturgy.

Although Fr Bugnini did not attend this North American congress, he did give a report on it. On the other hand, he played an important part in the First International Congress on Pastoral Liturgy a few weeks later in Assisi; it took place September 18–21, 1956. This congress was organized by the French, German, and Swiss centers for pastoral liturgy, which also invited the CAL to participate. There were meetings divided by language group to address specific issues as well plenary sessions. Altogether, there were about 1,100

---

7. The official proceedings of this conference present no such list; under the title "Resolutions" are found thanks and acknowledgements to Pius XII, Bishop Cody of London, the members of the London diocesan liturgical commission, Liturgical Conference Secretary (1952–1957) Fr Aloysius Wilmes, the mayor of London, and members of the media; *People's Participation and Holy Week: 17th North American Liturgical Week, London, Canada, August 20–23, 1956* (Elsberry, MO: The Liturgical Conference, 1957), 150. Proceedings of later liturgical weeks organized by the Liturgical Conference do not mention the list either. Yet a text of this list, signed by Fr Aloysius Wilmes in the name of the directors of the Liturgical Conference, was distributed at the First International Congress of Pastoral Liturgy held at Assisi, Italy, September 18–22, 1956 where *Documentation catholique* picked it up and published it in French translation (from the English): "Les vœux du Congrès liturgique de l'Amérique du Nord," *Documentation catholique* 1236 (14 October 1956): 1299–1301. The author, Yves Chiron, is drawing on this French translation.—*Trans.*

participants under the presidency of Cardinal Cicognani, prefect of the Congregation of Rites. Several outstanding representatives of the Liturgical Movement gave talks: Fr Jungmann, Dom Capelle, Msgr Wagner, and Dom Rousseau.

The theme of the Congress was "The Renewal of Pastoral Liturgy during the Pontificate of Pope Pius XII." Its intention was to take stock both of already implemented reforms and of those expected for the future. For instance, Cardinal Lercaro gave a talk on the simplification of the rubrics and on the reform of the breviary and made very concrete proposals, which were taken up later on by the conciliar preparatory commission. Several presentations also addressed the issue of the introduction of the vernacular into the liturgy. At the Congress, the preference was to speak of "living" languages, implicitly as opposed to Latin, in this perspective a dead language. After the Congress, Bishop Charrière of Lausanne, Geneva, and Fribourg referred to its work in a report he addressed to the *Commissio Piana*:

> The expression "living" language was preferred to the adjective "vulgar." You can easily see how pejorative the adjective "vulgar" is; but I believe that to consider whatever language is currently in use to be the only living language, while Latin is (to this way of thinking) a dead language, is already a false start. It is for us to see to it that Latin should not be a dead language, but that it remain a living language. We ought not to take it for granted that Latin is dead and in need of a substitute. I believe it is possible to involve the faithful in the Latin liturgy gradually, as has been done in many of our parishes where, for a long time now, we've been able to interest 90% of the faithful in the Latin liturgy.[8]

He pleaded, prophetically, in favor of retaining Latin:

> I daresay that it would be a great sorrow for priests and the faithful, in regions where they have successfully lived the Latin liturgy for a good long time, to abandon all that patrimony to try to become familiar with a vulgar-language liturgy. Since dechristianized regions are, alas, numerous and extensive, it may be that the

8. Report by Bishop Charrière dated September 14, 1956, in *Memoria sulla Riforma liturgica*, 99.

Holy See will come to the point of having to grant broad concessions in the area of the so-called living language. I earnestly beg,
however, that the dioceses and regions that deem themselves capable of keeping the Latin liturgy for the fore-Mass and the Sacraments may keep this Latin liturgy undisturbed, with the option of
translating certain parts of the Mass.

The most striking text connected with the Assisi Congress is the
long speech Pius XII gave the day after it ended. On September 22,
1956, he welcomed Assisi Congress delegates to the Vatican in the
presence of several cardinals and hundreds of bishops. He gave a
long allocution, in French.[9] He first hailed the Liturgical Movement
"as a sign of the providential dispositions of God for the present
time, as a movement of the Holy Ghost in the Church, to draw men
more closely to the mysteries of the faith and the riches of grace
which flow from the active participation of the faithful in the liturgical life."

He then wished to "treat some important questions which are
coming up for discussion today in the field of liturgy and
dogma...." He recalled the Holy See's authority in liturgical matters, "since it belongs to the popes to examine current forms of worship, to introduce new ones, and to regulate the arranging of
worship, and to the bishops to watch carefully that the canonical
prescriptions relating to divine worship are observed."

A large portion of the allocution was devoted to the then much-
debated question of concelebration. Concelebration was quite cir-
cumscribed at the time: during priestly ordination Masses and the
consecration of bishops. Some communities and liturgists were asking for an extension of the practice. Concelebration as community
Mass had been the object of many debates. Pius XII and the Holy
Office had had to intervene on several occasions to define what a

9. Pius XII, Address "Vous Nous avez demandé" to the International Congress
on Pastoral Liturgy, AAS 48 (1956): 711–25; English translation, "Allocution," *The
Assisi Papers. Proceedings of the First International Congress of Pastoral Liturgical,
Assisi–Rome, September 18–22, 1956* (Collegeville, MN: Liturgical Press, 1957), 223–
36.

sacramental concelebration is. Already in 1954, during an allocution made to cardinals and many bishops, he had condemned certain erroneous ideas on the subject:

> An assertion that is being made today, not only by laymen but also at times by certain theologians and priests and spread about by them, ought to be rejected as an erroneous opinion: namely, that the offering of one Mass, at which a hundred priests assist with religious conviction, is the same as a hundred Masses celebrated by a hundred priests. That is not true.[10]

During a week-long session of liturgical studies organized by a partnership between the CPL and the Liturgical Institute of Trier (whose director was Msgr Weber) at Mont César Abbey in 1954, the question of concelebration was once again discussed. The participants had disagreed on the concept of concelebration: the Germans deemed that silent participation around the altar could be considered a valid concelebration. Pius XII, in his speech to the Assisi Congress delegates in 1956, specified the nature and extent of concelebration: the words of consecration must be uttered by each of the priests at the altar[11] and concelebration must be distinguished from the "community Mass" in which priests attend a Mass said by another.

In the 1956 allocution, Pius XII also broached a long-debated subject: the use of the "vulgar tongue" in the liturgy. Although substantial concessions had already been granted, the pope reaffirmed the following: "The Church has grave reasons strenuously to maintain the unconditional obligation for priests in the Latin rite to celebrate in the Latin language; likewise, when Gregorian chant accompanies the Holy Sacrifice, it must be in the language of the Church."

At the very same time, Bishop Martin of Rouen, president of the French bishops' commission on pastoral concerns and theology,

---

10. Pius XII, Address "Magnificate Dominum" to Cardinals, Archbishops, and Bishops Gathered in Rome for Ceremonies in Honor of Our Lady, *AAS* 46.15 (18 November 1954): 669; English translation, *The Pope Speaks* 1 (1954): 375–85, at 378.

11. The Holy Office, in a reply published May 23, 1957, declared the concelebrated Mass to be invalid when only one of the concelebrating priests says the words of consecration aloud, *L'Osservatore Romano*, 25 May 1957.

addressed a letter to the Congregation of the Holy Office in the name of the Assembly of Cardinals and Archbishops of France (the A.C.A.) to request a broadened use of French at Mass. On October 11, 1956, Cardinal Pizzardo, secretary of the Congregation of the Holy Office, granted to all the dioceses of France the reading or chanting of the Epistle and of the Gospel in French after their being read or chanted in Latin; on the other hand reading "only in the vulgar tongue," even at Low Masses, remained forbidden.[12]

Week-Long Study Sessions

During the Assisi Congress Fr Bugnini had floated the idea of organizing yearly week-long sessions devoted to liturgical study and *aggiornamento* for seminary liturgy professors and students in Italy. In Italy at the time there did not exist a university-level institute specializing in the liturgy, such as existed in other countries: the *Institut Supérieur de Liturgie* in France, the Liturgical Institute of Trier in Germany. Archbishop Alcini, the Italian seminary visitator who attended the congress, gave his approval to the idea when Fr Bugnini proposed it to him.

By January 1957, Fr Bugnini had established a program and sent out invitations. The first *Settimana di studio per i professori dei seminari* took place the following July 7–14. It brought together about seventy liturgy professors at the Leoniano, the Vincentian headquarters in Rome. Besides the above-mentioned Archbishop Alcini, there were Cardinal Pizzardo, prefect of the Sacred Congregation for Seminaries, and Archbishop Confalonieri, secretary of the Sacred Consistorial Congregation (the Congregation of Bishops).

Therefore, besides the liturgical study weeks for the general run of the clergy that the CAL had been organizing since 1949, there were from 1957 on week-long liturgical study sessions for professors. This initiative was to continue during the years to follow; then, in

---

12. The response was published in *La Semaine religieuse d'Autun, Châlon et Mâcon*, 24 November 1956 and in *Documentation catholique* 1240 (9 December 1956), 1561.

1960, Fr Bugnini, who was too busy at the preparatory commission on the liturgy, handed over the task of organizing these week-long sessions to the *Centro di Azione Liturgica* (CAL), which has kept them going to the present day.

5

The Liturgy on
the Eve of the Council

I N JANUARY 1959, John XXIII announced the convocation of an ecumenical council. A few months later an Antepreparatory Commission was established under the direction of the Secretary of State, Cardinal Tardini. Among other things, this commission surveyed the bishops of the whole world as well as religious order superior generals to discover their *vota* ("wishes") concerning the topics to be addressed, the questions they wished to see discussed in the upcoming Council.

The Antepreparatory Commission received 2,109 responses.[1] Reforms concerning the liturgy are topmost among the "wishes" expressed by the bishops.

For example, Cardinal Montini, Archbishop of Milan (and future Paul VI) expressed himself bluntly. In his *vota*, he wrote that he wished "to give back to Christian piety its theological and biblical foundation, to moderate unhealthy forms of piety turned towards various and often arbitrary devotions that run against liturgical piety and an authentic religious sense." Cardinal Montini, like a certain number of other bishops, also declared himself in favor of "boldly" introducing living languages into the liturgy and reducing the role of Latin.[2]

---

1. These were published in the *Acta et Documenta Concilio Œcumenico Vaticano II apparando*. Series I (*Antepraeparatoria*), vol. II, *Consilia et vota episcoporum et praelatorum* (Vatican City: Typis Polyglottis Vaticanis, 1960–1961).

2. Yves Chiron, *Paul VI*, 2nd ed. (Versailles: Via Romana, 2008), 152.

Pierre Jounel, who studied the responses of the 84 French sitting bishops, indicates that 51 of them dealt with liturgical issues:

> Among them only sixteen ask for a certain extension of the vernacular; three wish for the issue to be addressed at the Council; two are formally opposed to it for the Mass. . . . The desire for the use of French concerned mostly the readings at Mass and the celebration of the sacraments. Some asked for the possibility of saying the entire Mass of the Catechumens in French. Only one, the bishop of Orleans, wished the entire Mass, except for the Canon, to be celebrated in the living language.[3]

It is worth noting that only three *vota* (those of the German bishops' conference, of the archbishop of Strassburg, and of the archbishop of Zaragoza) ask for the restoration of communion under both kinds.

After the responses had been received in Rome, a Central Preparatory Commission was established, as were specialized commissions. On June 5, 1960, a preparatory commission for the liturgy ("De sacra liturgia") was created. It was tasked with preparing a draft (*schema*) for a constitution on the liturgy to be presented to the Council and discussed there. Cardinal Gaetano Cicognani, prefect of the Congregation of Rites, was named its president and Fr Bugnini, its secretary. He was truly to be the architect of the commission's work, as Cardinal Cicognani—who would die on February 5, 1962—was not present at every meeting.

This preparatory commission's work was known in part, especially that concerning the use of the vulgar tongue in the liturgy.[4] The entirety of the documents, available in the Vatican Secret Archives (ASV), has now been published by Fr Angelo Lameri, liturgy professor at the Pontifical Lateran University.[5] He has pub-

---

3. Pierre Jounel, "Genèse et théologie de la constitution *Sacrosanctum Concilium*," *La Maison-Dieu* 155 (1983): 9.

4. See Monika Selle, "Latein und Volkssprache im Gottesdienst. Die Aussagen des Zweiten Vatikanischen Konzils über die Liturgiesprache" (PhD diss., Munich Faculty of Catholic Theology, 2001).

5. Angelo Lameri, *La "Pontificia Commissio de Sacra Liturgia Praeparatoria Concilii Vaticani II": Documenti, Testi, Verbali* (Rome: Edizioni Liturgiche, 2013); henceforth Lameri.

lished the introductory reports to the discussions and the minutes of the various work sessions during which the *schema* and its succeeding drafts were worked out (April 1961, August 1961, November 1961, and January 1962). This is an essential resource and can be supplemented by the accounts that various participants in the events have published.

The Influence of the Liturgists

The commission originally consisted of twenty-one members and thirty-three consultors. Deaths, replacements, and further nominations brought the total figure to sixty-three. While the pope officially named the members and consultors, there were many interferences. When the first list of members and consultors was published on August 26, 1960, it included no French or German bishop—that is, no bishop from the countries at the cutting edge of the Liturgical Movement. Furthermore, it included neither Msgr Wagner, director of the Liturgical Institute of Trier, nor the two kingpins of the CPL, Fr Roguet and Canon Martimort.[6] The secretary, Bugnini, successfully had them nominated by October 24 (later, in Fr Roguet's case).[7]

In the commission *De sacra liturgia* as in other preparatory commissions, the distinction between member and consultor was no mere formality, since the members alone had the floor in the plenary sessions. There were bishops and priests in both groups, however, and the consultors did not play a secondary role. Both members and consultors participated in the discussions and meetings and even had a voice (orally or through written reports), although only the members had a vote in the plenary sessions. In point of fact, reading the debates one realizes that the consultors intervened just as much as the members, if not more; the distinc-

---

6. A.-M. Roguet, "Le Centre de pastorale liturgique," in *Mens concordat voci. Mélanges offerts à Mgr A.-G. Martimort* (Paris: Desclée de Brouwer, 1983), 379.

7. On 8 March 1961, three further members (Fr Roguet among them) and two further consultors were named.

tion between the two would become even more blurred when the subcommissions were established, as we shall see.

As a matter of fact, there was no opposition between the members and the consultors. One finds bishops among the consultors as well as among the members, and one also finds liturgy experts (professors or authors of liturgical studies) both among the members and among the consultors.

The commission was intended to represent the universal Church. Among the members one finds a bishop of the Chaldean church in union with Rome, an African bishop, and a Brazilian bishop and, among the consultors, an Indian bishop. Yet the vast majority of the members and consultors belonged to the European clergy.

Out of sixty-three members and consultors, only thirteen were bishops; the predominance of the experts was manifest. One also notes the predominance of religious (thirty-five, mainly Benedictines, Dominicans, and Jesuits) over secular priests (twenty-eight).

A number of representatives of the Liturgical Movement were on this commission, whether as members or as consultors. All were old acquaintances of Fr Bugnini's: the Belgian Benedictines Bernard Capelle and Bernard Botte; the Austrian Jesuits Josef Jungmann and his disciple Johann Hofinger; Msgr Wagner, director of the Liturgical Institute of Trier; and several Frenchmen, including the Dominican Pierre Gy, Canon Aimé-Georges Martimort, and Sulpician Pierre Jounel. Although he was not a representative of the Liturgical Movement as such but shared its concerns, one notes the name of the Oratorian Bevilacqua, who had been one of Paul VI's teachers at Brescia and was created cardinal in 1965. Most of them would end up in the postconciliar commission in charge of implementing the liturgical reform intended by the Council. One of them, Dom Bernard Botte, was later to say: "These teams had already worked together for over ten years. The constitution on the liturgy was supposed to be the outcome of the Liturgical Movement."[8]

---

8. Bernard Botte, *From Silence to Participation. An Insider's View of Liturgical Renewal*, trans. John Sullivan (Washington, DC: Pastoral Press, 1988), 122 (adapted). Fr Roguet said as much: "Le Centre de Pastorale Liturgique," 379.

Bugnini was pleased with the freedom of the debates and with the confrontation of different points of view: "The contribution made by cultural background and by experience was quite clear. Local views and local situations evoked the sensitivity of others and helped to refine thought, expression, and emphases."[9]

A Preparatory Survey

The first sessions of the preparatory commission on the liturgy took place on November 12 and 15, 1960. One month earlier, on October 13, Fr Bugnini had sent to each of the members and consultors a lengthy survey to prepare for the meetings. This survey had been formulated by the board of the secretariat (*Consiglio di Segreteria*), which was made up of the Secretary (Fr Bugnini), the *minutante* (Vincentian Fr Braga, a collaborator of Fr Bugnini's for several years), the editor/archivist (Fr Giovanni Tautu), and two consultors, Fr Ansgar Dirks, a Dutch Dominican, and Fr Eugène Cardine, a French Benedictine.[10]

The survey was evidently drawn up from different sources: the above-mentioned consultation of the bishops of the world, the questions that had been left untreated by the *Commissio Piana* mentioned above, and also concerns specific to Fr Bugnini and his collaborators.

The *Quaestiones* sent out in October were distributed into twelve sections, each of which included several questions or topics to be dealt with:[11]

I. *De missa* ("Is it necessary or opportune to revise the Mass in its totality, or only certain parts? In its texts? In its ceremonies?" etc.).

II. *De concelebratione sacramentali* (on concelebration).

9. Bugnini, *Reform*, 18.

10. Dom Eugène Cardine (1905–1988), monk of Solesmes, professor at the Pontifical Institute of Sacred Music since 1952. He remains famous for the controversy that opposed him to the Gregorian chant theories of his predecessors at Solesmes, Dom Mocquereau and Dom Gajard, starting in 1957.

11. See Lameri, 57–65 for a synopsis of the survey in its different versions (between October and November 1960).

III. *De Officio divino* (on the breviary and the monastic office).

IV. *De sacramentis* (on the revision of the sacraments of baptism, confirmation, extreme unction, and marriage).

V. *De calendario recognoscendo* (on the revision of the liturgical calendar, "a disciplinary, not a dogmatic, issue").

VI. *De lingua latina* (on liturgical language and the possible "concession" of the vernacular in the Mass, the other sacraments, and the Divine Office, "in what parts and to what extent?").

VII. *De institutione liturgica* (on the teaching of the liturgy in seminaries and faculties of theology).

VIII. *De fidelium participatione in sacra liturgia* (on the "participation" of the faithful and the ways of applying it to the Mass, the sacraments, and sacramentals).

IX. *De liturgiae aptatione ad traditionem et ingenium populorum* (on the adaptation of the liturgy to the cultures and traditions of different peoples).

X. *De sacra supellectile, vestibus et ornamentis liturgicis* (on liturgical furnishings, vestments, and ornaments).

XI. *De musica sacra* (on sacred music, Gregorian chant, "under what conditions" modern music and "popular religious songs" may be allowed in the liturgy).

XII. *De arte sacra* (what principles and rules ought to guide sacred art and "what are the forms to be rejected for sacred art?").

While certain questions seem to concern rather generic subjects ("on liturgical furnishings and ornaments," "on sacred art"), others bore upon themes that had been written about and discussed over the course of several years in specialized journals and liturgical congresses: concelebration, the revision of the liturgical calendar, the introduction of the vernacular in the liturgy, and the "participation" of the faithful.

A subcommission would ultimately be set up for each of these disputed questions. During the preparatory commission's first meeting on November 12, 1960, Bishop Jenny, an auxiliary bishop of the Archbishop of Cambrai in northern France, observed that "the whole point was missing: before any reform or revision of the various liturgical books, the Council needed first of all to present the doctrine [of the liturgy]."[12] A new subcommission was therefore created; it was called *De Mysterio sacrae liturgiae eiusque relatione ad vitam Ecclesiae* ["On the mystery of the liturgy and its relation to the life of the Church"]. It became the first among the thirteen subcommissions; Fr Bevilacqua was named as its relator, Fr Martimort as its secretary, and Bishop Jenny, Fr Jungmann, and Dom Cannizzaro, Benedictine abbot of the Genovese monastery, as consultors.

The solemn opening ceremony of the Council's preparatory phase took place on November 14 in Saint Peter's Basilica. All of the preparatory commissions' members gathered around John XXIII, who gave an allocution. The very next day the liturgy commission met a second time and the membership of each of the thirteen subcommissions was settled. Each was composed of a relator, a secretary, and between three and six consultors.[13] Some of the consultors belonged to several subcommissions, such as Dom Botte who sat on the subcommission *De lingua latina* (which subcommission was more commonly and significantly called the "living language" subcommission) as well as on the subcommissions on concelebration and liturgical instruction.

Each subcommission had four months, with a deadline set at March 15, to study the problem it had been assigned and to submit proposals to the general session for examination. Some subcommissions were very active and met several times while others met only once or even not at all. The subcommissions did not necessarily meet in Rome. For instance, the first subcommission held its first meeting in Brescia, where Fr Bevilacqua was pastor, then at the French seminary in Rome. The subcommission on concelebration met only once, in Fribourg (one of its members, Fr Hänggi, was professor there at the time). The subcommission devoted to liturgi-

---

12. Aimé-Georges Martimort, "Padre Giulio Bevilacqua (1881–1965) e la riforma liturgica conciliare," in *L'impegno religioso e civile di P. Giulio Bevilacqua* (Brescia: CEDOC, 1983), 85.

13. See Lameri, 54–55, for the subcommissions' memberships.

cal instruction never met, some of the members merely sending in reports.

Fr Bugnini orchestrated the whole and coordinated the subcommissions. Dom Botte praised his work:

> I want to be sure to mention my admiration for the man who organized all the work, Father Bugnini. He is one of those modest workmen who remain offstage, but without whom nothing would get done. His position as secretary was difficult and delicate. National susceptibilities had to be dealt with, while safeguarding the quality and level of the work. It was desirable, in fact, to invite liturgists of different countries to collaborate in the reform; but nationality was not a criterion of competence, and an eye had to be kept on seeing that the various problems were treated by the best qualified people.[14]

Most of the subcommissions worked out texts and *vota de reformatione* ("proposals for reform"), which were examined, discussed, and amended in the commission's plenary session, April 12–26, with two meetings a day.

Who Is the Authority in Liturgical Matters?

Without going into the detail of all the "proposals for reform" (*vota de reformatione proposita*) contained in these early texts, it is worthwhile to point out the more salient *vota* among them, the discussions they occasioned during the plenary session, and the role Fr Bugnini played in them. We shall also highlight other proposals made during the discussions and to what extent they were adopted for the first draft of a constitution on the liturgy.

Among the very first points to be discussed was the bishops' authority in the future liturgical reform.[15] The original text under examination stated at the outset: "A greater freedom is to be left to the bishops in regulating the sacred liturgy." Bishop Rossi of Biella raised an objection against "the danger of this broader freedom" granted to bishops in this matter, since this might jeopardize "the

14. Botte, *From Silence to Participation*, 118–19.
15. During the November 12, 1960 session; Lameri, 41–42.

unity of the manifestation of the life of the Church." Bishop Zauner of Linz proposed that "such a faculty ought to be granted to bishops' conferences rather than to individual bishops." Another member, Bishop Hervás, seconded by the Italian Benedictine consultor Cannizzaro, made the case that a broad freedom left to the bishops was not suitable if it concerned liturgical legislation (*in ferendis legibus*), but that it was acceptable if it was for "the application of universal law to the needs and circumstances of different regions." Brazilian Bishop Nabuco pointed out that the Code of Canon Law in its wisdom "leaves to the Holy See alone the regulation of the liturgy; quite often the bishops are not experts in the liturgy and have no such experts available." Fr Jungmann, for his part, considered that "the new legislation ought to grant greater powers to the bishops' conferences, leaving to the bishops the regulation of private devotions."[16]

This was not an insignificant question, as the answer to it would determine whether the liturgical reform to come would be decided or controlled entirely by the Holy See, or a certain freedom in making decisions and applying the reform would be left to the local level (the diocese or the bishops' conference).

The Second Vatican Council, after many a debate, would establish general norms maintaining the Holy See's authority in liturgical matters, leaving certain powers to bishops' conferences within certain "limits" while denying simple priests any power in the matter:

1. Regulation of the sacred liturgy depends solely on the authority of the Church, that is, on the Apostolic See and, as laws may determine, on the bishop.

2. In virtue of the power granted by the law, the regulation of the liturgy within certain defined limits belongs also to various kinds of competent territorial bodies of bishops legitimately established.

16. The custom at the time was to distinguish "liturgical actions," i.e., acts of worship according to the liturgical books approved by the Holy See, from "private devotions," which are "other sacred actions performed either in the church or outside of it," but not defined in a ritual established by the Holy See.

3. Therefore, no other person, even if he be a priest, may add, remove, or change anything in the liturgy on his own authority.[17]

The extent to which the last of these norms was breached is well known.

Latin and Living Language

The use of Latin in the liturgy and the introduction of modern languages ("living" or "vernacular languages") were also discussed.

The norms on the matter were not old since they had been recalled and specified in the Instruction of the Congregation of Rites dated September 3, 1958 presented above. This Instruction had recalled that "Latin is the language of liturgical ceremonies," but that "in private devotions any language more suited to the faithful may be used." It specified:

> In sung Masses, only Latin is to be used. This applies not only to the celebrant and his ministers, but also to the choir or congregation. . . . At low Mass, the faithful who participate directly in the liturgical ceremonies with the celebrant by reciting aloud the parts of the Mass that belong to them must, along with the priest and his server, use Latin exclusively.

But a good many members of the preparatory commission thought it possible to go further. A good number of bishops, theologians, and liturgists encouraged them in this direction. During a meeting of the first subcommission in Brescia, Cardinal Montini hosted about ten consultors in Milan on February 9, 1961 at Fr Bevilacqua's suggestion. According to one of the participants, Fr Gy, the man who was to be Paul VI spoke "right away about the vernacular as something to which he had given much thought and which he deemed to be important: 'I think that the time is ripe.'"[18]

The work of the preparatory commission gave rise to conjectures in the press and in various circles on the abandonment of Latin. On

---

17. *SC* 22.

18. P.-M. Gy, "Mgr Bugnini et la réforme liturgique de Vatican II," *Revue des sciences philosophiques et théologiques* 69.2 (April 1985): 315.

March 25, 1961, an anonymous article came out on the front page of *L'Osservatore Romano* to defend Latin ("Latino, lingua della Chiesa").

Fr Bugnini then acted with prudence. The seventh subcommission, which was specifically in charge of the Latin language, had prepared a long and rather daring *relatio* that was supposed to have been presented and discussed during the April 1961 plenary session. Fr Bugnini managed to convince the relator, Msgr Pietro Borella, to withdraw his report. He gave assurances that it would be better to give scattered indications throughout than to devote a whole chapter to the subject.[19]

Nevertheless, a discussion did take place on April 13.[20] Fr Valerio Vigorelli, consultor and specialist in sacred architecture, deemed that "for reasons of artistic unity, all the parts that are said aloud in liturgical celebrations ought to be in the same language. In practice, for the Mass, in the vulgar tongue; for the Office, in Latin." Bishop Malula shared this opinion.

Canon Martimort questioned this analysis and pointed out that "history attests to the simultaneous use of several liturgical languages" and was of the opinion that it was up to the bishops' conferences to resolve the problem. Another consultor, the Belgian Norbertine Fr Boniface Luykx, pointed out that "in mission territories a broader use of the vulgar tongue must be granted. Most often the Latin language is perceived as a vestige of colonialism."

Bishop Calewaert of Ghent expressed a balanced view: "It is certainly necessary that the vulgar tongue be employed for the didactic part of the Mass. But Latin must remain in order to foster unity and for travelling foreigners. It must therefore remain the principal language of the Ordinary of the Mass."

Msgr Higinio Anglés, director of the Pontifical Institute of Sacred Music—who was to oppose Bugnini over sacred chant, as we shall see—warned that "an indiscriminate concession" of the vernacular in the liturgy would jeopardize sacred chant, which is in Latin. Dom

---

19. Bugnini, *Reform*, 24 and Lameri, 324.
20. For the text of the *Propositio*, see Lameri, 417–21; for the *Verbale* of the April 13, 1961 meeting, see ibid., 109–12.

Capelle, OSB, while agreeing to a broader introduction of the vulgar tongue in the liturgy, nevertheless pointed out "the danger there would be in excluding Latin in regions where there are two or more official languages" (he was specifically alluding to Belgium, his own country).

Lastly, by decision of the preparatory commission president, Cardinal Cicognani (who was absent), only general considerations were retained. The cardinal did not want excessively concrete proposals to be made and stir up controversy on the outside. In the final draft of the constitution, it was reaffirmed that Latin remained the language of the "western liturgy," while a broader use of the vernacular for the readings, exhortations, chants, and prayers was asked for. The decision and the determination of the proportion of vernacular (*eligendi modum et mensuram usus linguae vernaculae*) was left up to the choice of each region's episcopal conference.

Shortly after the preparatory commission on the liturgy had completed its task, John XXIII published the Apostolic Constitution *Veterum Sapientia*.[21] In it, he reasserted, following Pius XI, that the Church needs "a language which is universal, immutable, and non-vernacular." John XXIII also defined Latin as "a most effective bond, binding the Church of today with that of the past and of the future."

The Structure of the Mass

Both in the preparatory work of the subcommission on the Mass and in the plenary session discussions, there was no dearth of proposals for the reform of the Mass; they provoked many a debate.

The proposed *schema* as well as the amended *schema* asserted as a general principle that the "structure" of the "so-called Mass of Saint Pius V" had to be "reformed" in such a way that additions be suppressed (*ut additiones supprimantur*) and that other elements be improved or embellished (*elementa genuina ac fundamentalia ac*

---

21. Apostolic Constitution *Veterum Sapientia*, 22 February 1962. For a contextual and philological analysis, see Alberto Melloni, "Tensioni e timori alla vigilia del Vaticano II: la costituzione apostolica *Veterum Sapientia* di Giovanni XXIII (22 febbraio 1962)," *Cristianesimo nella storia* 11.2 (June 1990): 275–307.

tempori nostro convenientia excolantur, "elements genuine, fundamental, and suited to our times should be cultivated").

At no time, it seems, did any participant (member or consultor) ever propose—at least publicly—the addition of other canons to the sole Roman Canon then in use. Some, however, were proposing that changes ought to be introduced into it.[22] Dom Vagaggini suggested granting the faculty of "introducing one or two local saints" among those named in the Canon. Fr Jounel suggested that the celebrant recite the entire Canon aloud. The Austrian Jesuit Fr Hofinger asserted that "there ought to be no prohibition against changing something in the Canon," which earned an immediate rejoinder from his confrere (and former professor) Jungmann: "but those changes ought to occur only for the gravest reasons." Fr Roguet suggested abolishing the signs of the cross before the final doxology in the Canon, but that this doxology ought to be chanted (*Per ipsum...*). Canon Martimort suggested that the *Pater* ought to be sung by all the faithful along with the priest, "though *sotto voce.*"

Once again members and consultors suggested that no specific proposal be retained as such and indicated that proposals could be handled during the Council or in the postconciliar commission in charge of applying the Constitution as approved by the Council.

Nevertheless, there are very concrete proposals in the successively produced general *schemas*: the significant reduction of "signs of the cross, kisses at the altar, genuflections, bows, and other things of this type" (*rariores fiant in Missa crucesignationes*, etc.); the expansion of the Offertory rite (with a "procession of the gifts"); the simplification of the communion formula; the expansion of communion under both species "for clergy and religious as well as for the laity ... in specifically determined circumstances according to the judgment of the bishops."

The Question of Concelebration

The question of concelebration was discussed during the April 14, 1961 meeting, in which an introductory report, given by Dom Ber-

---

22. *Verbale* of April 13, 1961; Lameri, 112, 115–16.

nard Capelle on behalf of the third subcommission, was discussed.[23] Several members judged that this practice of concelebration (until that time essentially reserved to Masses in which priests were ordained or bishops consecrated) could be extended (*extendi potest*). Dom Vagaggini asked that "the theological reasons" for concelebration should be added to the draft. The American Benedictine Diekmann judged it "desirable" for concelebration to be extended to conventual Mass, "so that it may clearly appear as the summit of the day's liturgical worship." Canon Martimort pointed out that in Saint Athanasius's church in Rome [the church of the Greek college, where the Byzantine rite is celebrated], there already was concelebration every day: "Why couldn't it be the same in churches where there are several priests?" Fr Jungmann approved and added: "likewise in houses of studies" (*etiam in scholasticatibus*). Nevertheless, Fr Roguet voiced the following objection: "But it should be clearly stated that concelebration is not obligatory, so that there may still be personal celebration for the sake of convenience or devotion, except on Maundy Thursday."

In the amended *schema*, the preparatory commission expressed the wish that the use of concelebration be extended to conventual Masses, to the principal Mass when there are several priests, in houses of studies, in houses where spiritual exercises are given, in religious houses where pilgrims are hosted, and during extraordinary celebrations with the bishop (diocesan synods and pastoral visitations). This is exactly what the Council was to ask for.

Inculturation

The term "inculturation" only appeared in 1975. Yet the intention is already apparent in the work of the conciliar preparatory commission. The tenth subcommission ("On the adaption of the liturgy to the traditions and character—*ingenium*—of peoples") was tasked with preparing a *schema*. During the April 1961 plenary session, before the *expositio* of the titular relator, American patrologist John Quasten, Fr Bugnini gave the floor to the commission's only Afri-

---

23. *Verbale* of April 14, 1961; ibid., 120–24.

can, Bishop Malula. This auxiliary bishop of Leopoldville in the Belgian Congo presented a *relatio* that was far more trenchant than Quasten's report following it.[24] While acknowledging that Westerners had been "instruments of Divine Providence" in bringing the Gospel to Africa and bringing her into the Church, Bishop Malula questioned the "foreign" liturgy, "which does not correspond to the basic needs of our peoples." He judged that the Roman liturgy, "by dint of its legalism and sobriety," was opposed to (*contradicit*) the "spontaneity, sense of movement, and solemnity of our populations."

Without going into the detail of the discussion that followed, it is worth noting the distinction drawn by Fr Hermann Schmidt, professor at the Gregorian University: a) *aptatio ad ingenium populorum*; b) *assimilatio usuum gentium*; c) *christianisatio usuum gentium*. He judged that the reports that had been presented so far dealt rather with the first point (adaptation) than with the second (assimilation) and third (Christianization).

Indeed Bishop Malula's presentation had once again opened up the issue of the "inculturation" of the liturgy (an old debate if one recalls the long Chinese Rites controversy). Once he was named archbishop of Kinshasa and created cardinal by Paul VI in 1969, he would promote the "Zairean rite," which has been among the most accomplished (and controverted) expressions of the africanization of the liturgy.

The Liturgical Year and the Revision of the Liturgical Calendar

The revision of the liturgical calendar was among the subjects that had long been discussed by certain liturgical specialists. The subcommission dealing with this issue first tackled whether or not to establish a fixed date for Easter. Fr Roguet frankly opposed it, deeming it to be a "mathematical idea," while other members and consultors were in favor. The proposal was taken up again in the final draft of the constitution on the liturgy: "that the feast of Easter be fixed

---

24. Bishop Malula, *Relatio*, ibid., 176–77.

on a determined Sunday," in agreement with the "separated brethren" (the Orthodox).

More globally, however, the preparatory commission on the liturgy endeavored to determine a "liturgical year" that would give preeminence to the Temporal over the Sanctoral, i.e., bringing out the Proper of the Season, the feasts celebrating the important steps in the life of Christ (birth, death, resurrection, etc.). In this perspective, Sunday, the day "of the celebration of the Paschal mystery and of the regeneration of the Christian people's faith," was defined as "having a particular nature." "Other celebrations [viz., of the saints], unless they be truly of greatest importance, shall not have precedence over" it.

This formula, as found in the three successive *schemas* (August and November 1961, January 1962) would end up verbatim in the conciliar Constitution (*SC* 106).

The desire was for a revision of the entire liturgical year: "The minds of the faithful must be directed primarily toward the feasts of the Lord whereby the mysteries of salvation are celebrated in the course of the year. Therefore, the proper of the time shall be given the preference which is its due over the feasts of the saints."[25]

Lest saints' days (the Sanctoral) should take precedence over the Temporal, the preparatory commission asked "that most of them should be left to be celebrated by each particular church or nation or religious family, only those commemorating saints of truly universal relevance being extended to the Church universal."[26]

This entailed the disappearance of a large number of Saints from the universal calendar.

The Divine Office

The fourth subcommission was in charge of the "Divine Office." This term had been preferred to "breviary." This subcommission also held working meetings with the preparatory commission *De*

25. This proposal in the final schema (n. 83; Lameri, 743) will be found verbatim in the conciliar Constitution (*SC* 108).

26. Note 86 of the final schema; Lameri, 757, 759.

Religiosis on February 17 and 18, since secular and religious priests shared the Divine Office.

There had long been an aspiration for the reform of the breviary, as we have seen. To a great extent, the subcommission took over the work of the *Commissio Piana* on the subject. The *schema* envisaged a structural reform of the Divine Office.[27] The office of Matins was renamed the *Officium Lectionum* because a greater share of it was to be given to the readings. It would be composed of six or three psalms and three readings (two drawn from Sacred Scripture and one from the Fathers of the Church or Lives of the Saints) every day. These readings were to be "longer and more varied, in such a way that the priest may find in them material for daily meditation." Excerpts from the Martyrology were to be added to Lauds. The Office of Prime was to be suppressed "because it constitutes a monastic duplication of Lauds." The three Little Hours (Terce, Sext, None) were each to be reduced to a hymn and a psalm, or even suppressed and replaced with a single office termed *Media contracta*, made up of a hymn and three psalms. Everyday an *Oratio fidelium* was to be added to Vespers in the form of prayers said for the Church's general needs.

The *schema* also dealt with the issue of language. Asserting that "the Divine Office in choir must be celebrated in the Latin language," it nevertheless provided for two exceptions: "If a significant part of the choir—especially among nuns—or if the lay faithful who participate in the Office do not understand Latin, the use of another language may be granted." The bishop or the bishops' conference was to take the decision.

The conciliar Constitution took over the substance of this *schema* on the Divine Office.

Lay Participation

We have seen that fostering lay "participation" in liturgical worship, particularly in the Mass, was one of the Liturgical Movement's major concerns in general, and indeed was present in many of Fr Bugnini's writings and initiatives since the 1940s.

---

27. *Nota sul nuovo schema proposto per l'Ufficio divino*, presented April 17, 1961; ibid., 166–67. For the revised schema see ibid., 278–90.

The *schema* proposed by the first subcommission already contained a proposal to make "the participation of the faithful more active and conscious." The proposal was that in every celebration a deacon or "commentator" should explain what the priest was doing with "short commentaries" and "guide" the prayer of the faithful.[28] This idea had been taken over from what Fr Bugnini had experimented with and advocated in his "paraphrased Mass" of 1950—a practice that the September 1958 Instruction allowed.

The preparatory commission did not adopt this proposal. On the other hand, it did adopt the principle that all readings from the Sacred Scriptures in the Mass should be made "in a language that all the faithful understand," a principle that was already widespread at the time.

The relator of the ninth subcommission, which was specifically dedicated to this theme of participation, was Dom Cannizzaro, an old acquaintance of Fr Bugnini's. The first meetings took place starting in November 1960 at Saint Anselm's Abbey, on the Aventine. Then Cannizzaro's unexpected death on March 14, 1961 had led to the nomination of a new relator, Fr Roguet, OP.

In his *relatio* introducing the *schema* for discussion, Fr Roguet had made ample reference to Pius XII's encyclical *Mediator Dei*. Reading the minutes of the discussions themselves, which took place in April 1961, one realizes that the conversation had less to do with defining this participation than with points of detail that might have been better addressed elsewhere. Reducing the number of feasts was brought up, as well as introducing new Masses for other feasts, which led Msgr Higinio Anglés, president of the Pontifical Institute of Sacred Music, to exclaim: "If new Masses are introduced, don't forget the music." Fr Fischer suggested changing the title of the feast of the Purification of the Blessed Virgin Mary to the Presentation at the Temple (which in fact the postconciliar *Consilium* did). Fr Kahlefeld suggested making a sharp distinction between the "Liturgy of the Word" and the "Liturgy of the Sacraments," which would indeed appear clearly in the new *Ordo Missae* of 1969. Fr Pascher suggested suppressing a proposed Mass for bap-

28. Lameri, 229–31.

tism (*Missa in celebratione Baptismi*), as he deemed that the celebration of the sacrament during the Sunday Mass was sufficient.

The theme of lay participation is also to be found in another *schema*, that dealing with the sacraments and sacramentals. It contained the request that the formulas of all sacramental rites, "except those of the Eucharist and Holy Orders," should be "recited by the minister in the vernacular."

Discussions on Sacred Music

The discussions on sacred music, April 21–22, 1961, may have sparked the liveliest debates within the preparatory commission. There was an opposition between two conceptions that was to last well after the Council.

The subcommission in charge of studying the question and preparing a draft had Msgr Higinio Anglés, president of the Pontifical Institute of Sacred Music since 1947, as relator. Certain members and consultors wanted a broad introduction of vernacular songs into the liturgy to foster lay participation. Others, particularly Msgr Anglés, deemed that Gregorian chant, because of its antiquity and purity (i.e., its sobriety), is better suited to the sacred character that ought to adorn all liturgy and is the music most prone to fostering piety and elevating the soul.

Although no member or consultor on the commission wanted to do away with chant altogether, some thought it was necessary to end its predominance. The defenders of Gregorian chant faced a stiff opposition during the discussions.[29] An Australian, Percy Jones, music director for the diocese of Melbourne and choirmaster of Saint Patrick's cathedral in Melbourne, asserted: "There has to be a double liturgy (*duplex liturgia*): one for cathedrals and monasteries, the other for the parish." Dom Vagaggini asked to "make the principle of a need for a sacred music subordinate to the principle of lay participation." Canon Martimort warned against the danger of "archeologism" and asked "that new melodies be composed with prudence, according to the needs of the liturgy and the evolution of

---

29. *Verbale* of the meetings on April 21–22, 1961; Lameri 197–208.

the musical arts." Fr Moneta asserted that "the Gregorian is a dead language, just like Latin." Fr Luykx drew from his experience as a missionary the conclusion that "monosyllabic Gregorian chant ... is not enough for those populations that want rhythm and musical instruments" and he deemed it necessary to admit to the liturgy, for "those populations," "wind and percussion instruments" (*sive flatu sive percussione sonant*).

Msgr Anglés was among the only ones to defend the legitimacy and universality of "the artistic treasure of the Church" that was Gregorian chant. He petitioned: "If it pleases the Council to grant that Gregorian chant be combined with modern languages, let this be only in the case of poetical texts, not other texts."[30]

Discussions relative to the report of the thirteenth and last sub-commission, which dealt with sacred art and architecture, occasioned various proposals.[31] Canon Martimort suggested that in the future, when it comes to building churches, the "best rule" ought to be set down, namely that the tabernacle ought not to be set up above the high altar but rather on a separate altar.

The proposal of the American Benedictine Fr Diekmann was more revolutionary: "let the altar facing the people be authorized" (*ut permittatur altare versus populum*). The conciliar Constitution on the Liturgy did not make a pronouncement on this specific suggestion, but by 1965 it had become the norm!

Three Successive *Schemas*

The preparatory commission's plenary meeting ended on April 24, 1961. After the several *vota* expressed during the meetings, Fr Bugnini prepared an initial *schema* (draft) of a constitution on the liturgy. He integrated the *vota* into the preparatory texts and reorganized the whole in eight coherent and consistent chapters.

The first general redaction of the *schema* was sent to all the members and consultors on August 10, 1961. They had a month to express any possible "observations." There were about 1,500 of them, mostly

---

30. See also his *Votum*, Lameri, 395.
31. *Verbale* of the April 22, 1961 meeting: Lameri, 208–13.

dealing with the first chapter. This brought about the need to organize a new meeting of the first subcommission to work out a new redaction of this first chapter. It took place October 11–13, 1961 at Domus Mariae. Then, on November 15, Fr Bugnini was in a position to send a second version of the general *schema* to all the members. There were 752 further amendments yet. Consequently, at the new plenary meeting, January 11–13, 1962, a third draft of a constitution was examined and one last time corrected in the presence of Cardinal Cicognani, commission president.

The official text of this third draft was handed to Cardinal Cicognani on the following January 22. Bugnini would later say that the Cardinal received this text "with joy and trepidation. As always when he had to make a binding decision, he hesitated and wanted to reread the text."[32] Fr Bugnini did not hide that he had a few fears himself: "If Cardinal Cicognani had not signed the Constitution, the result, humanly speaking, would have been a real disaster. Everything would have had to be discussed all over again."

Cardinal Cicognani finally signed the *schema* on February 1 and sent it on to the Central Preparatory Commission.

The Bugnini Method

The preparatory commission on the liturgy had finished its work. When one reads the *verbatim* minutes of its plenary meetings, one notes few interventions from the secretary, Fr Bugnini. At the meetings, he allowed the members and consultors to express themselves freely and never voiced an opinion specific to himself. The most he ever did was to bring a meeting to a close with general considerations or a methodological instruction.

In the rather short history of this preparatory commission (June 1960–January 1962), Bugnini was manifestly a peerless organizer and manager. Supposing that he had his own opinion on all the subjects under discussion, he nonetheless never sought to impose his own views.

On the other hand, he did have a concrete influence through the

32. Bugnini, *Reform*, 25.

regular contacts he had with members and consultors before and after the plenary meetings. The proposed introduction of a "commentator" into the liturgy, as we have seen, certainly came from him, even though someone else presented it. Since it was not adopted in the successive drafts, he evidently was not all-powerful within this preparatory commission.

Nevertheless, what may be termed "the Bugnini method" clearly emerges in this preconciliar period. On the one hand, it consists in having groups of experts work separately on restricted subjects and having the members vote during very few plenary meetings (the Committee had only three: November 12–15, 1960; April 1961; and January 11–14, 1962). On the other hand, it also consists in refraining at the outset from excessively bold proposals that might be rejected at the Council and putting certain questions and reforms off until later, after the Council. *Remittatur quaestio post Concilium* ("Let the question be postponed until after the Council") is a recurring note during the discussions of the preconciliar commission.

Fr Bugnini himself presented his method before a small number of members and consultors during the previously mentioned November 11, 1961 meeting at the Domus Mariae:

> It would be most inconvenient for the articles of our Constitution to be rejected by the Central Commission or by the Council itself. That is why we must tread carefully and discreetly. Carefully, so that proposals be made in an acceptable manner (*modo acceptabile*), or, in my opinion, formulated in such a way that much is said without seeming to say anything: let many things be said in embryo (*in nuce*) and in this way let the door remain open to legitimate and possible postconciliar deductions and applications: let nothing be said that suggests excessive novelty and might invalidate all the rest, even what is straightforward and harmless (*ingenua et innocentia*). We must proceed discreetly. Not everything is to be asked or demanded from the Council—but the essentials, the fundamental principles [are].[33]

---

33. Fr Bugnini, Declaration opening the October 11, 1961 meeting; Lameri, 433.

6

"First Exile" During the Council

C ARDINAL GAETANO CICOGNANI had signed the draft of the constitution on the liturgy on February 1, 1962, as we have seen. He sent it on to the Council's Central Preparatory Commission, which was to examine it and communicate it to the bishops of the whole world.

A few days later, February 5, Cardinal Cicognani died. Spanish Cardinal Larraona, of the Claretians, succeeded him as prefect of the Congregation of Rites. It was he who presented the *schema* on the liturgy before the Central Preparatory Commission.

As the opening of the Council was nearing, Fr Bugnini expected to be put in charge of the secretariat of the conciliar commission on the liturgy, just as he had been for the preparatory commission. Archbishop Felici, secretary general of the Council, called him in on October 6, 1962. He informed him that Fr Antonelli, of the Franciscans, the promotor general of the Faith at the Congregation of Rites and former member of the *Commissio Piana*, was going to be named secretary of the conciliar commission for the liturgy.

Bugnini was beyond surprised. On the morrow, he wrote to Archbishop Felici to tell him his disappointment and his hope that he might yet be named:

> This fills me with bitterness. I am still hoping for a reasonable solution. I have worked with enthusiasm and sacrifice for two years. . . . The discrimination that causes me and the commission offense also offends against the memory of Card. Cicognani, who had put all his trust in me, and it casts a shadow on my reputation.[1]

---

1. Bugnini to Archbishop Felici, 7 October 1962, in Bugnini, *Memorie*, 69.

On the same October 6, or the next day, he received a letter from Antonio Piolanti, rector of the Pontifical Lateran University, informing him that "on orders from the Holy See," the class on pastoral liturgy he had been teaching at that university since 1957, as we have seen, was being withdrawn from him. Piolanti was a representative of what has been called "Roman theology," which is characterized by its attachment to the Magisterium and a theological tradition derived from Saint Thomas Aquinas. The decision he took to withdraw from Fr Bugnini his teaching post at the Lateran was doubtless not a personal one. It seems to have stemmed from the mistrust of Bugnini that had spread in various circles.

This double sacking had a profound effect on Fr Bugnini: "I saw him weep," reported Canon Martimort.[2] Bugnini tried to find out who had given this order, "but I never was able to find out," he wrote.[3] Nevertheless, Bugnini did learn what was held against him. Fr Bisoglio, procurator general of the Vincentian congregation, went to see the various dicastery authorities, especially Cardinal Larraona, the new prefect of the Congregation of Rites. The latter justified his decision to remove Fr Bugnini: "Fr Bugnini is excessive (*è troppo spinto*)." In the presence of other interlocutors Cardinal Larraona also called him an "iconoclast" (*iconoclasta*).[4] Dom Bernard Botte, who had been a member of the preparatory commission and became a member of the postconciliar *Consilium*, wrote: "Some members of the Curia were displeased with the *schema*, which they considered too progressive, and they directed their bad feelings against Father Bugnini."[5]

Other preparatory commission members, such as Fr Bevilacqua, were not called to the conciliar commission either. Nonetheless, Fr Bevilacqua, like Fr Bugnini, was included in the official list of Council *periti* ("experts") and they were able to follow the discussions from the box reserved for experts. They also continued to

2. A.-G. Martimort, "La Constitution sur la liturgie de Vatican II. Esquisses historiques," *La Maison-Dieu* 157 (1984): 43.

3. Bugnini, *Memorie*, 58, where he gives October 7 as the date on which he learned of this double eviction.

4. As reported by Archbishop Bugnini himself, ibid., 73.

5. Botte, *From Silence to Participation*, 123.

exert their influence through the meetings and conversations that were multiplying *extra aulam.*

The situation was soon to be reversed. Indeed, at this time Fr Bugnini made the acquaintance of Cardinal Montini, the future Paul VI, who was the archbishop of Milan at the time and had come to Rome to take part in the Council. Fr Bevilacqua, a longtime friend of Montini's, brought the two men together. They met on November 8, 1962. Cardinal Montini "asked in great detail" about the reasons for Bugnini's deposition and brought up the *schema* of the liturgy constitution, which was then under discussion.

Sometime later, Cardinal Montini and Cardinal Lercaro, Archbishop of Bologna, tried to plead Bugnini's case. In his own memoirs Bugnini reports that the two cardinals went together to see the Secretary of State, Cardinal Amleto Cicognani, to "protest," as they considered that Fr Bugnini's non-nomination in the liturgy commission was a "first attempt on freedom at the Council."[6] Cardinal Cicognani—brother to Cardinal Gaetano Cicognani who had been president of the preparatory commission on the liturgy—gave assurances "that he would refer it to the Holy Father." But if the matter was ever submitted to John XXIII, he did not intervene to have Bugnini named to the conciliar commission and if, perhaps, he asked Fr Piolanti to take Fr Bugnini back as professor at the Lateran, the request remained without effect.

From *Schema* to Constitution

The liturgy *schema* was examined by the Second Vatican Council in its very first session (October–December 1962). In his memoirs, Fr Bugnini speaks of this period as his "first exile" (the second one being his definitive exile to Tehran in 1975). The expression is an exaggeration, however. Fr Bugnini was among the Council's official *periti* (experts). As such he was able to attend all of the Council's sessions from the box reserved to experts, as we have seen. Furthermore—although he does not mention it in his memoirs—thanks to Fr Antonelli he was named as *peritus* in one of the liturgy commis-

---

6. Bugnini, *Memorie*, 69.

sion's thirteen subcommissions, that on "General Observations."[7] Also, one of Bugnini's close collaborators, Fr Carlo Braga, was one of Fr Antonelli's assistants in the liturgical commission secretariat.

Bugnini was therefore able to follow closely the elaboration of the Constitution on the Liturgy, *Sacrosanctum Concilium*. Many members of the preparatory commission on the liturgy had become members of the conciliar liturgical commission, such as Canon Martimort. Fr Bugnini continued to be in close contact with many of them and they would exchange information. As Canon Martimort reports, "every day he communicated to me useful information and warned me of the maneuvers that were being plotted in various quarters."[8]

Fr Bugnini also had several opportunities to share his observations at a higher level.

The *schema* on the liturgy was the only one prepared before the Council that the Council Fathers did not reject. It came under examination during the fourth general congregation, on October 22, 1962.[9] That day twenty-five Council Fathers spoke on the subject. Without going into details regarding the various arguments they made, it is worth pointing out that in this matter as in all the subjects discussed at the Council, the cardinals' and bishops' speeches *in aula* (i.e., during the general congregations in Saint Peter's Basilica) are not sufficient to take the full measure of every development, change, and conflict. Equally influential was what I have termed the "peri-Council,"[10] that is to say, the *extra aulam*

---

7. Giampietro, *Development*, 77.

8. Martimort, "La Constitution," 44.

9. In addition to the *Acta Synodalia*, the official publication of the discussions at the Council, Fr Giovanni Caprile's lengthy chronicle, *Il Concilio Vaticano II* (Rome: La Civiltà Cattolica, 1966–1969), 6 vols., is a treasure-trove of information [henceforth Caprile]. [For a detailed account in English, see G. Alberigo and J. A. Komonchak, eds., *History of Vatican II*, vol. 2, *The Formation of the Council's Identity. First Period and Intersession, October 1962–September 1963* (Leuven: Peeters, 1997).]

10. Yves Chiron, "Paul VI et le péri-concile," in *La papauté contemporaine (XIXᵉ–XXᵉ siècles)*, ed. J.-P. Delvillle and M. Jakov (Louvain: Bibliothèque de la Revue des Études Ecclésiastiques/Vatican City: Archivio Secreto Vaticano, 2009), 585–603.

communications, which operated along different lines (lectures, meetings, books, articles) and involved nearly countless actors (not only cardinals and bishops, but also *periti*, theologians, and journalists).

For instance, Brazilian Bishop Isnard, later a member of the postconciliar *Consilium*, has pointed out the importance of the regular meetings on the liturgy during the Council's first session at Villa Mater Dei on the Viale delle Mura Aurelia. Canon Martimort "never missed one":

> The great liturgical experts were in attendance: Fischer, Wagner, Jungmann, Gy, Franquesa, Oñatibia, as well as some bishops such as Van Bekkum, Volk, and others. Hermann Volk, bishop of Mainz, usually presided over the proceedings, during which everyone spoke in his own language, Gy being the German-French interpreter. The Spaniards and Latin Americans spoke French.
>
> Our meetings, which were highly interesting, supported the progress that the Constitution draft was making in the general congregations and within the conciliar commission on the liturgy. We'd get plenty of information and we organized talks. We had to be vigilant against the efforts of the conservative opposition and fight for the approval of certain of the Liturgical Movement's demands such as the use of the vernacular, which was the main concern at the time.[11]

At the Council, the first twenty-five speeches *in aula* on the liturgy *schema* were perforce brief, no more than a few minutes. Therefore, some of the speakers gave their arguments in greater detail elsewhere and sought to reach a broader audience by using different means of communication. For instance, Cardinal Montini, the archbishop of Milan, took the floor on the very first day of the debate on the liturgy to "approve the *schema* openly" and to plead for "an extended use of the vernacular." To his mind, the matter was urgent: "If we do not want [the faithful] to leave the churches . . . the obstacle of a language," i.e., Latin, which few amongst them understood, had "to be removed." Furthermore, it was "necessary to

---

11. Clemente José Carlos Isnard, "Le 'Consilium,'" in *Mens concordat voci. Mélanges offerts à Mgr A.-G Martimort* (Paris: Desclée, 1983), 405.

simplify and shorten the ceremonies." In tandem with this, the archbishop addressed a public letter to his diocesan priests in which he further developed the argument: "The liturgy is not esoteric . . . it is a language." In liturgical celebrations, "there ought to be room for the living language in the didactic and euchological parts."[12]

The debates on the liturgy *schema* went on during the following days. An incident occurred at the tenth general congregation on October 30. The secretary of the Congregation of the Holy Office, Cardinal Ottaviani, became aggressive in a speech that was so long that the session president cut him off after fifteen minutes.[13] At the outset he expressed his concern over an expression in the *schema*: "What does *ordo missae . . . recognoscendus* [the ordo of the Mass is to be revised] mean? Now, is a sort of revolution of the entire Mass desired? . . . What will remain of it?"

Then, though without naming him, he seems to have been aiming at Fr Bugnini when he noted that communion under both kinds was mentioned in article 42 and concelebration was mentioned in article 44 even though the majority of the Central Commission, over which Ottaviani presided, had rejected both a few months before. He was denouncing a maneuver and deemed that the text as provided to the Council was not the same as that to which the Central Commission had granted its approval.[14] The cardinal was openly opposed to the extension of these two practices. Regarding communion under both kinds, he denounced "a veritable itch for novelty, which insists on things that are not only not necessary, but also not even useful and may even be dangerous." Regarding concelebration, he stated: "It is a certain external—don't blame me if I say theatrical—form of celebrating the Mass, and here too there is the danger of error."

Fr Bugnini felt that this accusation of doctoring texts was aimed at him. He wrote a letter of protest to the president of the Council's

12. 27 October 1962 letter, in Montini, *Lettere dal Concilio*, 32–33.
13. *Acta synodalia Sacrosancti Concilii Oecumenici Vaticani II*, I, Periodus Prima, pars II (Rome: Typis Plyglottis Vaticani, 1970), 18 and Caprile, 2.103–4. [See also Mathijs Lamberigts, "The Liturgy Debate," in Alberigo and Komanchak, *History of Vatican II*, 126.]
14. Ibid.

administrative tribunal, Cardinal Francesco Roberti. He pointed out that the articles that had been put back into the *schema* after the Central Commission had examined it had been put there after a decision on the part of the subcommission for amendments. A few days later, Cardinal Confalonieri, president of that subcommission, confirmed in a general congregation that the contested articles had indeed been reintroduced pursuant to their examination by the body over which he presided.[15]

The examination of the liturgy *schema* continued over the next few days. On November 8, as we have seen, Fr Bugnini met Cardinal Montini for the first time. During this meeting the Archbishop of Milan asked Fr Bugnini "why the work of the conciliar commission [on the liturgy] was not moving forward and how it could be put back on track so as to end the first session of the Council with a vote on the liturgy *schema* and allow the Fathers to go home with something positive in hand."[16]

Cardinal Montini asked Fr Bugnini to provide him with a memorandum on the subject. On their end, Canon Martimort and Cardinal Lercaro too were hard at work. Martimort recalled that

> the commission is made powerless by its president [Cardinal Larraona] who seems bent on keeping it from working. I alerted several bishops, who presented him with a fruitless petition on November 9; Cardinal Lercaro sent the Secretariat of State a memo on November 11 describing the situation.[17]

In fact, work on the *schema* was well under way. According to Fr Caprile's account at the time, from the fourth to the eighteenth general congregation (October 22–November 14), there were 325 interventions *in aula* on the *schema* (some cardinals and bishops intervening more than once), plus 360 written interventions given

---

15. *Acta Synodalia* I.II., 106–8 and Caprile, 2. 113–14. [See also Lamberigts, "The Liturgy Debate," 131.]

16. Bugnini, *Memorie*, 75–76.

17. A.-G. Martimort, "Le cardinal Giacomo Lercaro (1891–1976). Souvenirs d'un liturgiste," in *Mirabile laus canticum. Mélanges liturgiques, études historiques, portraits de liturgistes* (Rome: Edizioni Liturgiche, 1991), 380.

directly to the Council secretary, which also had to be taken into account.

The first vote took place during the nineteenth general congregation on November 14, 1962 at the initiative of Cardinal Tisserant, president of the Council. This did not concern approving the *schema* as a whole or any of its chapters; it was about approving its guidelines (*criteria directiva*). In the Council's terminology, it was an orientation vote. There were 2,162 *placet* out of 2,215 votes. This vast majority in favor of a *schema* that was still under examination was very encouraging, especially since it was the first time a text was voted on at the Council.

Fr Bugnini wrote a letter to Cardinal Tisserant on the very day of the vote to thank him for his initiative. He manifestly took this first vote as a personal victory, or at least as the approval of the work the preparatory commission had done. He wrote, in slightly awkward French: "In the joy of a first success I beg you to kindly accept the liveliest and most grateful thanks, also in the name of the preparatory commission on the liturgy, which I am sure of representing, for the decision and dynamism with which you have led the conciliar session this morning."[18]

After this first vote of approval, the Council went on to examine another *schema*, that on Revelation (which was to become the Constitution *Dei Verbum*). For its part, the liturgy commission continued its work. The first definitive texts, which had been changed in light of the previous weeks' interventions and amendments, were presented in a general congregation and successively submitted to the Council Fathers' votes. Consequently, on December 7, 1962 (36th general congregation), at the end of the first session, a definitive vote on the preamble and first chapter of the Constitution on the Liturgy took place. Once again, the result was unambiguous: of 2,118 votes, 1,992 voted *placet*, only eleven *non placet*, to which were added 180 *placet juxta modum* (approval subject to modifications) and 5 invalid votes.[19]

---

18. Fr Bugnini to Cardinal Tisserant, 14 November 1962. Archives of the *Association des Amis du Cardinal Tisserant*.

19. Caprile, 2.264. See also Lamberigts, "The Liturgy Debate," 166.

Fr Bugnini was delighted with this first step, a "success" (as he wrote to Cardinal Amleto Cicognani) which "shows that the preparatory commission had chosen the right path and had interpreted the bishops' wishes correctly." In the same letter, he persisted in his desire for rehabilitation and asked the Secretary of State for the measures that had been taken against him to be lifted, so that his "honor" and "reputation" might be restored.[20] He received no answer.

Anticipations and Experiments

Although the Constitution on the Liturgy had not yet been wholly adopted, liturgical innovations were multiplying in a number of dioceses. In an unparalleled ferment of high expectations (which ferment more or less authoritative voices and a great many of the media in Europe and elsewhere fostered with their declarations), bishops and especially priests took unevenly felicitous initiatives, thereby getting ahead of the changes that were to be decided at Rome. The Guinean Cardinal Robert Sarah, named prefect of the Congregation for Divine Worship and the Discipline of the Sacraments in 2014, recounted what he witnessed in his own country in late 1962 or early 1963, when he was still a seminarian and the Constitution on the Liturgy had not yet been promulgated:

> The cathedral of Conakry had an elegant, ornate choir, with a beautiful replica of the Bernini baldachin, surrounded by very beautiful angels. At the time of the first discussions about liturgical reform, Archbishop Tchidimbo returned to Conakry and ordered the destruction of the baldachin and the main altar. We were angry, incredulous at this hasty decision. Rather violently, we passed without any preparation from one liturgy to another.[21]

In France, too, initiatives and experiments were multiplying. Several bishops had to intervene to ask for a "status quo"[22] or to warn

---

20. Bugnini to Cardinal Amleto Cicognani, 16 December 1962, in Bugnini, *Memorie*, 76–77.

21. Robert Sarah, *God or Nothing: A Conversation on Faith*, trans. Michael Miller (San Francisco: Ignatius Press, 2015), 84.

22. Cardinal Feltin, Archbishop of Paris, in *La Croix*, 20 December 1962.

against those who were playing at being "precursors" or indulged in "fanciful innovations."[23] Consequently, the assembly of cardinals and bishops of France had to publish a note on March 15, 1963 forbidding "liturgical anticipations":

> Pursuant to the discussion on the liturgy *schema* undertaken during the first session of the Council, the Assembly of Cardinals and Archbishops has decided to specify that nothing is to be changed in the current norms and disciplines until the definitive adoption and official promulgation of the new texts. Any anticipation would be imprudent and unjustified. Under the present circumstances, it would constitute an infraction that could be prejudicial to its authors and jeopardize rather than serve the cause of the liturgy.[24]

The Conciliar Constitution *Sacrosanctum Concilium*

John XXIII died a few months later, on June 3, 1963. Cardinal Montini was elected pope on June 21 and took the name Paul VI. Bugnini, who as we have seen had been in contact with him since November 1962, knew that the new pope was determined to continue the Council and the reform of the liturgy.

Indeed, the second session of the Council opened in late September of 1963. The examination of the liturgy *schema* resumed straightaway. It went on, chapter by chapter, until the end of November. During the seventy-fifth general congregation (November 22, 1963), the *schema* on the liturgy was approved as a whole by 2,159 yes votes against 19 no votes. Then, after a final vote on December 4, 1963 (2,147 *placet* vs. four *non placet*), the Constitution on the Liturgy, titled *Sacrosanctum Concilium*, was promulgated by Paul VI.

Without getting into an exhaustive analysis of the document, one can give it a synthetic presentation by noting that its dominant theme is the need not only for a renewal of the liturgy as a whole but

---

23. Archbishop Weber of Strasburg, in *La Croix*, 4 April 1963.
24. This note was published in various diocesan weeklies and in *Documentation catholique* 1399 (5 May 1963): 617–18.

also for a reform of the Mass. The critics who, after the adoption of the *Novus Ordo Missae*, said that the Council had never asked for a reform of the liturgy were wrong. On the other hand, it is true that the reform that Archbishop Bugnini had prepared and that Paul VI promulgated went beyond what the Council had contemplated, if not what it had desired. It may be said that the postconciliar reform did not fundamentally betray what the Council wanted, but what we have here is doubtless what the sociologist Jules Monnerot called 'heterotely': an end (*telos* in Greek) has diverged from what was originally intended. The Council had expressed its wishes and the *Consilium* in charge of applying the conciliar Constitution did so by implementing a systematic program.

The conciliar Constitution did ask for a complete revision of the rites (n. 50):

> The rite of the Mass is to be revised in such a way that the intrinsic nature and purpose of its several parts, as also the connection between them, may be more clearly manifested, and that devout and active participation by the faithful may be more easily achieved. For this purpose the rites are to be simplified, due care being taken to preserve their substance; elements which, with the passage of time, came to be duplicated, or were added with but little advantage, are now to be discarded; other elements which have suffered injury through accidents of history are now to be restored to the vigor which they had in the days of the holy Fathers, as may seem useful or necessary.

The conciliar Constitution does not establish a complete list of the reforms to be undertaken. It keeps to wishes and recommendations without detailing applications, although it does give some rather precise indications: a greater diversity of Scripture readings (n. 51); higher esteem for the homily (n. 52); restoration of the common prayer (n. 53); communion under both kinds (n. 55); and concelebration (n. 57).

The conciliar text does not envisage the use of the vernacular in the liturgy for the entire Mass, but only for some of its parts, and wants Latin to remain the liturgical language (n. 36): "Particular law remaining in force, the use of the Latin language is to be preserved in the Latin rites." It is likewise provided that Gregorian chant, since it is "specially suited to the Roman liturgy ... should be given pride of place in liturgical services" (n. 116).

Bugnini noted with some satisfaction that "no substantial changes were made" between the *schema* that the preparatory liturgical commission had prepared and the definitive and solemn text of the conciliar Constitution on the Liturgy as Paul VI promulgated it.[25] Indeed a comparison between the January 1962 *schema* and the December 1963 Constitution reveals no essential difference.[†]

The final text of the Constitution on the Liturgy was voted in by the near-unanimity of the Council Fathers. Even Archbishop Lefebvre, who was to become a determined opponent of the Second Vatican Council and the great defender of the "perennial Mass," voted for the text. Although he soon regretted "unforeseen and infelicitous results," at the time he recognized that a reform of the liturgy was necessary, including in the Mass:

> There was something to reform and to rediscover. Clearly, the first part of the Mass, which is intended to instruct the faithful and for them to express their faith, needed to reach those ends in a clearer and so to speak more intelligible manner. In my humble opinion, two such reforms seemed useful: first the rites of that first part and also a few translations into the vernacular.
>
> The priest coming nearer to the faithful; communicating with them; praying and singing with them and therefore standing at the pulpit; saying the Collect, the Epistle, and the Gospel in their language; the priest singing in the divine traditional melodies the *Kyrie*, the *Gloria*, the creed with the faithful: these are so many good reforms that give back to that part of the Mass its true finality.[26]

---

25. Bugnini, *Reform*, 27.

  [†] It is noteworthy, however, that all of the citations of preconciliar magisterial documents (e.g., *Mediator Dei*) with which earlier iterations of the Constitution were liberally annotated, were removed right before the final text was voted on. See Susan Benofy, "Footnotes for a Hermeneutic of Continuity: *Sacrosanctum Concilium's* Vanishing Citations," *Adoremus Bulletin* 22.1 (Spring 2015): 8–9.—*Ed.*

26. Marcel Lefebvre, "Perspectives conciliaires entre la 3ᵉ et la 4ᵉ session," *Itinéraires* 95 (July–August 1965): 78–79.

Rehabilitation

Paul VI had a clear vision, not of every step and detail of the reform, but of the means to implement it. He decided not to entrust this task to the Congregation of Rites, as one might have expected, but to a specific and independent organism.

By September 11, 1963, when the Constitution on the Liturgy had not yet been voted on, Cardinal Lercaro had already announced to Fr Bugnini by letter in a somewhat mysterious tone: "Truth always ends up imposing itself with its own evidence. I hope to see you again soon; I'll have something to tell you in person."[27]

On October 10, Paul VI mentioned the work of the Council's then-ongoing second session to the four cardinal moderators (Agagianian, Döpfner, Lercaro, and Suenens). There was reasonable hope that the examination of the Constitution on the Liturgy would soon be over. The pope wished for "a kind of transitional legal framework (*legge stralcio*)" to be drawn up with no further delay.[28]

The very next day, October 11, Cardinal Lercaro tasked Fr Bugnini under the seal of secrecy with constituting a study group to prepare this "transitional legal framework." For this new undertaking Fr Bugnini called upon several collaborators, nearly all of them former members of the preparatory commission: Fr Jungmann, Canon Martimort, Fr Schmidt, Dom Vagaggini, Fr McManus, Msgr Wagner, and Msgr Bonet. Bugnini thus returned, discreetly at first, to a central position in the work of liturgical renewal that was beginning in Rome.

The work would be done diligently but in the greatest secrecy in October–November. Two drafts were produced: a motu proprio (called *Primitiae*) determining a few elements and a more detailed instruction giving practical norms. They were finalized too late to be published before the end of the Council's second session, however. Their tone may also have been judged too bold or their proposals insufficiently developed.[29]

27. Lercaro to Bugnini, 11 September 1963, in Bugnini, *Memorie*, 77.

28. Bugnini, *Reform*, 54; Marini, 1–2.

29. Rainer Kaczynski, "Toward the Reform of the Liturgy," in *History of Vatican II*, vol. 3, 238–40.

It is possible that the pope ultimately decided that these documents were premature since they had been put together when the Constitution on the Liturgy had not yet been definitively voted on and promulgated. In his closing address at the end of the Council's second session, Paul VI merely announced the upcoming publication of "opportune and authoritative instructions" on the conciliar Constitution that had just been voted on and promulgated.

7

Secretary of the *Consilium*

A COMPARISON OF the different witnesses for this period indicates that for a few months from about December 1963 to March 1964 there were, at Paul VI's express wish, two parallel and competing projects for the implementation of the conciliar consitution on the liturgy. They were to merge into one, though not without some difficulty. Unlike what Bugnini's writings might lead one to believe, at the outset he was not considered to be the only man for the job.

By December 1963 Paul VI had tasked Fr Antonelli, secretary of the conciliar commission on the liturgy, to prepare a general plan for the revision of liturgical books and to define the organism responsible for it.[1] He worked in close collaboration with Cardinal Larraona, prefect of the Congregation of Rites. In a memorandum presented to Paul VI, Antonelli proposed a program consisting of fourteen work groups and a new commission reduced to five bishops and eight experts.

Meanwhile on January 3, 1964 Cardinal Cicognani, Secretary of State, in the name of Paul VI tasked Fr Bugnini with organizing a commission for the implementation of the Council's Constitution on the Liturgy.[2] Bugnini worked in close collaboration with Cardinal Lercaro. He had not yet finished the project when, on the following January 13, an official letter from the Secretariat of State announced the creation of a *Consilium ad exsequendam Constitutionem de Sacra Liturgia* (Committee for the Implementation of the

---

1. Bugnini, *Reform*, 60 and Giampietro, *Development*, 163–82.
2. Bugnini, *Reform*, 49–50, 61.

Constitution on the Sacred Liturgy).[3] At that date it numbered only three members, Cardinals Lercaro,[4] Giobbe, and Larraona, and a secretary, Fr Bugnini. Two days later at the first meeting of this *Consilium*, Fr Bugnini was in a position to propose an initial workplan. The *Consilium*, however, still only had a very undetermined status and ill-defined competencies.

Thus, there were two workplans, the Antonelli project and the Bugnini project; the two cardinals, Larraona and Lercaro, were rivals.

The Motu Proprio *Sacram Liturgiam*

The transitional legal framework on the liturgy, which as we have seen had been worked on since October 1963, was made public in two stages. First came a motu proprio, *Sacram Liturgiam*, dated January 23, 1964.[5] It is important to note that this motu proprio did not stem from the project prepared by Bugnini's small group in October–December of 1963. It had been prepared by Archbishop Felici, secretary general of the Council. This is another indication of Paul VI's hesitancy at this time regarding the implementation of the Constitution on the Liturgy.[6]

As Paul VI considered that "many of the prescriptions of the Constitution [on the liturgy] clearly cannot be put into effect in a short period of time, since some of the rites must first be revised and new liturgical books prepared," he deemed it necessary to publish certain "norms" that were "applicable now."

The short length of the motu proprio and the small number of the points it discussed (eleven articles, notably the liturgical formation of clergy, diocesan liturgical committees, the homily, confirmation,

---

3. The official creation of the organism and the first nominations were made public in *L'Osservatore Romano* the following January 31.

4. Cardinal Lercaro's name was listed first, but his rank as president of the new organism was not specified.

5. *L'Osservatore Romano*, 29 January 1964.

6. See Marini, 19–20, who underscores the coexistence of three projects of different origins.

marriage, the Divine Office) show that its goal was to satisfy—if only to a limited extent—those who were impatiently waiting for the liturgy to change while at the same time setting the necessary limits to the experimentations and innovations that were already multiplying in every country.

The motu proprio asked for the immediate preparation of liturgical studies curricula so that they might be implemented in seminaries and houses of studies at the beginning of the next academic year. It also asked for liturgy, music, and sacred art commissions to be established in every diocese. The obligation for the priest to give a homily at every Sunday and Holy Day of obligation Mass only repeated the conciliar Constitution's paragraph 52. The motu proprio did not wait for the reform of the breviary that the Council envisaged in allowing priests "to omit the hour of Prime and to choose from among the other little hours the one best suited to the time of day" and "to use the vernacular instead of Latin." It was also specified that bishops could dispense particular priests "from the obligation [to recite the Divine Office], in whole or in part" if it was "for just cause."

This motu proprio came as a disappointment to certain reformers, particularly Canon Martimort who had collaborated on the other draft for a motu proprio. He felt that "in its style, it disregards the spirit of the Constitution on the Liturgy."[7] Above all, however, a disposition regarding liturgical translations generated a heated controversy: the ninth article of the motu proprio stipulated that "the various vernacular translations proposed by the competent territorial ecclesiastical authority are to be revised and approved by the Apostolic See. This is the course to be taken whenever any Latin liturgical text is translated into the vernacular by the aforementioned authority."

This prescription set a limit on the authority of the episcopal conferences, which could only "propose" translations. The document seemed to fall short of what the Council had stated (*SC* 36.4): "Translations from the Latin text into the mother tongue intended

---

7. Martimort, "Le cardinal G. Lercaro," 383.

for use in the liturgy must be approved by the competent territorial ecclesiastical authority already mentioned."

"There was a huge uproar in the press and the episcopate," said Canon Martimort.[8] Bishops from various countries issued protests.

Paul VI, in a move he was to repeat under different circumstances when it came to the liturgy, agreed to modify the motu proprio. This time he entrusted the task to Fr Bugnini and the *Consilium*. The modified version of the document (including nineteen of Bugnini's twenty-one proposed changes)[9] therefore restored the authority of episcopal conferences in liturgical translation: the translations "must be drawn up and approved by the competent territorial ecclesiastical authority, as provided in art. 36, §3 and §4; and . . . as provided in art. 36, §3, the acts of this authority require due approval, that is, confirmation, of the Holy See."[10]

It is worth noting that the motu proprio nowhere mentions the rite of the Mass as such. In fact, on this specific point the Council's Constitution had expressed only an intention of reform without entering into detail. The motu proprio therefore did not prescribe any change in the matter. On the contrary, it ended with a warning that explicitly restated article 22 of the Constitution:

> Finally, we wish to emphasize that—beyond what we in this apostolic letter on liturgical matters have either changed or have ordered carried out at the established time—regulation of the liturgy comes solely within the authority of the Church: that is, of this Apostolic See and, in accordance with the law, of the bishop. Consequently, absolutely no one else, not even a priest, can on his own initiative add or subtract or change anything in liturgical matters.

8. Ibid. See also Bugnini, *Reform*, 58–59.

9. Marini, 26.

10. This, the revised version as published in the *Acta Apostolicae Sedis* 56 (1964): 139–44, will be found in *Documents on the Liturgy* 1963–1979: *Conciliar, Papal, and Curial Texts* (Collegeville, MN: The Liturgical Press, 1982), no. 287 (henceforth *DOL*). The first version translated above was published in *L'Osservatore Romano*, 29 January 1964, 1.

Rivalry with the Congregation of Rites

This motu proprio announced the creation of a "special commission whose principal task will be to implement in the best possible way the prescriptions of the Constitution on the Sacred Liturgy itself." The pope's January 25 motu proprio thus said "special commission"; the January 13 letter from the Secretariat of State had said *Consilium* ("committee"). In his extensive monograph on the liturgical reform, Archbishop Bugnini presents this difference of title as a simple uncertainty due to the beginnings of the new organization and its ill-defined competencies at the time.

In point of fact, it does seem that at the outset Paul VI had not made a definite choice between two possible lines: the Larraona/Antonelli line on the one hand and the Lercaro/Bugnini line on the other. In the early days of the *Consilium* different subjects and specific cases would provide occasions for rivalry, collaboration, or interaction between the Congregation of Rites, over which Larraona presided, and the new organization, which at first had no president.

Cardinal Larraona was listed among the first members of the *Consilium* at its creation in January 1964, as we have seen. The prefect of the Congregation of Rites may have considered that the *Consilium* was, as its name seemed to indicate, an "advisory committee" intended to do research and prepare draft texts, while the Congregation of Rites was to make the actual decisions.[11] He therefore set up a commission in February 1964 with Msgr Dante, secretary of the Congregation of Rites, as president; it met a few times at the Congregation's offices.[12] This group was to prepare a draft for a text on liturgical instruction to which we shall return.

At this time, therefore, there coexisted the *Consilium*, which according to Cardinal Larraona was merely advisory, and an executive commission that depended on the Congregation of Rites. A further question was the extent to which the *Consilium*, since it was tasked with "implementing" one of the Council's Constitutions, remained attached to the Council itself and to its governing bodies.

---

11. Bugnini, *Reform*, 51; Marini, 31.
12. Cf. Bugnini, *Reform*, 50 and Giampietro, *Development*, 164.

Archbishop Felici, who as secretary of the Council was regularly in contact with the pope, would also be a member of the *Consilium*.

Cardinal Lercaro and Fr Bugnini had no intention of operating under the aegis of the Congregation of Rites or under that of the Council's governing bodies; nor did they wish the *Consilium* to be a simple advisory committee. At the end of February 1964, Cardinal Lercaro wrote to Canon Martimort to share his concerns with him:

> I am deeply concerned by the attitude of the Congregation [of Rites]. It seems that the Congregation considers itself to be certainly in charge of the interpretation of the Constitution [on the liturgy], which in my opinion is not true. . . . In reality, I am quite anxious because of the unclear positions that are taking shape. I should like the *Consilium*—which is a postconciliar body—to be completely autonomous and especially not to depend at all on the Secretariat of the Council. Msgr Felici says this [dependency] is only in theory, but then, in practice, everything has to go through him.[13]

A few days later, on February 14, a large meeting took place under Cardinal Lercaro's presidency. Among the participants were Fr Bugnini, Secretary of the *Consilium*, and two other liturgical experts, Canon Martimort and Msgr Wagner, who had not yet been named to the new body. The topic of the meeting was the composition of the *Consilium*. Fr Bugnini had prepared a list of bishops and consultors to name as well as an organization chart of the future working groups. Bishop Isnard from Brazil, later a member, noted: "I have the impression that the choice of members for the *Consilium* was in large part suggested to Bugnini by Martimort; a subsequent confidence informed me that it was true in my case."[14] Canon Martimort later wrote: "That meeting determined the original outline of the *Consilium* and that of the actual implementation of the liturgical reform."[15]

13. Lercaro to Martimort (in Italian), 27 February 1964, quoted in Martimort, "Le cardinal G. Lercaro," 384–85.

14. Isnard, "Le 'Consilium,'" 406.

15. Martimort, "Le cardinal G. Lercaro," 385. Bugnini (*Reform*, 50) dates it to February 15 and does not name the participants.

The *Consilium*'s competencies were officially defined in the pope's name on February 29 through a letter from the Secretariat of State addressed to Cardinal Lercaro:

a. to suggest the names of the persons charged with forming study groups for the revision of rites and liturgical books;

b. to oversee and coordinate the work of the study groups;

c. carefully to prepare an instruction explaining the practical application of the motu proprio *Sacram Liturgiam* and clearly outlining the competence of territorial ecclesiastical authorities, pending the reform of the rites and liturgical books;

d. to apply, according to the letter and spirit of the Council, the Constitution it approved, by responding to the proposals of the conferences of bishops and to questions that arise involving the correct application of the Constitution.

Appeals of Consilium decisions as well as the solution of particularly sensitive and grave or completely new problems will be referred by the Consilium to the pope.[16]

Although the juridical status of the *Consilium* and its powers were not clearly and fully defined, it was not made dependent on the Congregation of Rites. From this point of view, the last paragraph was particularly important, as it stipulated that the Consilium need refer only to the pope himself as a last instance. Therein lay its strength. As Piero Marini, one of Bugnini's collaborators on the *Consilium*, pointed out, "ultimately the *Consilium*, unlike the dicasteries of the Roman Curia, was not bound by procedural habits or any specific regulations."[17]

Paul VI approved the nomination proposals. On March 5, *L'Osservatore Romano* published the complete list of *Consilium* members. Besides Cardinal Lercaro, now officially designated as president, the new body included nine other cardinals (among whom again Larraona), twenty-eight bishops, and four other members: Msgr Luigi

---

16. Letter quoted in Bugnini, *Reform*, 51.

17. Piero Marini, "Elenco degli 'schemata' del 'Consilium' e della Congregazione per il Culto divino," *Notitiae* 195–96 (October–November 1982): 459.

Valentini, Canon of St. Peter's Basilica (who died the following May); Dom Benno Gut, primate of the Benedictine Confederation; Fr Antonelli, who was integrated into the new body; and Fr Bevilacqua (whom Paul VI created cardinal a year later).

The composition of the *Consilium* was in stark contrast to the other curial bodies of the time: most of its members were residential bishops (bishops "in the field" as opposed to Vatican prelates) and the new body had an outstanding proportion of international members: the official announcement specified "forty-two members representing twenty-six countries on all continents." There were a Japanese bishop, an Australian bishop, five South American bishops, and so forth. The downside of this internationalization would be that the members would rarely all gather in Rome and that plenary sessions would number more consultors than members.

The task of this *Consilium* was "to prepare the general liturgical reform" and "to apply, according to the letter and spirit of the Council, the Constitution it approved." The order in which the tasks are presented is noteworthy: the application of the Constitution, which had already been drawn up, was mentioned after the elaboration of a future reform.

Cardinal Larraona, prefect of the Congregation of Rites, was concerned by this increasing autonomy being granted to the *Consilium*. He mentioned the situation in a conversation with Fr Antonelli, who then noted in his journal: "We are very saddened by the fact that the *Consilium* has arrogated to itself functions which logically inhered in the Congregation of Rites. The *Consilium* is a study organism: the Congregation is an organ of government."[18]

Rivalry and conflicts between the *Consilium* and the Congregation of Rites went on unceasingly.[19] At the pope's decision and after discussions from April to May 1964, the procedure for publishing future decrees was ironed out: they would be consigned by the cardinal prefect of the Congregation of Rites and the cardinal president of the *Consilium*.

---

18. Antonelli quoted in Giampietro, *Development*, 181, n. 15.
19. Bugnini, *Reform*, 71–80.

The commission that the Congregation of Rites had created was suppressed at Paul VI's decision.[20] The *Consilium* was indeed independent from the Congregation of Rites and operated under the direct authority of the pope. Soon Cardinal Larraona, a charter member of the *Consilium*, stopped attending its meetings. A higher authority had yet to intervene—in a letter from the Secretariat of State on January 7, 1965—to specify the respective competences of the *Consilium* and of the Congregation of Rites: the *Consilium* was given the study of questions, "experiments," the preparation of new liturgical books; the Congregation of Rites was given the promulgation of decrees (while the president of the *Consilium* added his signature to those too). At the same time Fr Bugnini, secretary of the *Consilium* since January 1964, was also named assistant secretary of the Congregation of Rites in January 1965 to establish his authority.

The *Consilium*'s Mode of Operation

This was no advisory committee; it was truly an autonomous decision-making body whose decisions and normative texts were ultimately subject only to the pope's approval.

The *Consilium*'s headquarters were established at Palazzo Santa Marta, behind St. Peter's Basilica. At first it took up two rooms. Its president, Cardinal Lercaro, usually resided in his archdiocese, Bologna. There were therefore only three people working at the Palazzo that first year: the secretary Bugnini, and two assistants: Vincentian Father Carlo Braga, a collaborator of his for many years, and a young religious, Fr Gottardo Pasqualetti of the Missionaries of the Consolata, who had just received his theology degree from the Pontifical University Urbaniana. Braga and Pasqualetti would remain Archbishop Bugnini's closest collaborators until his exile in Iran and they publish his personal writings to this day.[†]

Then, a year later, other collaborators hailing from different countries had to be recruited to deal with the increase in the *Consilium*'s activities. As its membership grew, the organism came to take

20. Ibid., 51.
† Fr Carlo Braga died on August 16, 2014.

up an entire story, the fourth floor of Palazzo Santa Marta. The *Consilium* also published a periodical. At first, in 1964, it was a modest mimeographed report, *Relationes*; then, from 1965, a printed journal, *Notitiae*, which published official texts (decrees, instructions, general presentations), information, and articles of an unofficial nature. The first issue was atypical (numbers 1–4, January–April 1965), but after that the periodical was a monthly publication.

Like every other Roman congregation, the *Consilium* had, besides its members (who would increase from 42 to 51 over time), a certain number of consultors (named by the Secretariat of State). Their number grew larger, far more than any other curial body. In his work, Bugnini provides a list of 149 names.[21] He also added a list (which as he specifies is not exhaustive) of unofficial "advisors" whom the *Consilium* consulted; this second list numbers 74 names. There was therefore an army of over 200 consultors and advisors spread across the globe who worked on the projects launched by the *Consilium*.

Consultors were charged with preparing drafts for examination in plenary session. They were divided up into a certain number of study groups (a total of 45), each with its own specialty.[22] While some subjects were the task of a single group (e.g., the revision of the Martyrology), others were distributed among several groups. For example, nine study groups worked on the reform of the breviary under the effective direction of Canon Martimort (who was also consultor for three other study groups). The revision of the *Ordo Missae*, which Msgr Wagner of the Trier Liturgical Institute directed, was distributed among seven study groups: the Ordinary of the Mass; Scripture readings at Mass; the Prayer of the Faithful; votive Masses; singing at Mass; the general structure of the Mass; concelebration; communion under both species.

Just as he had been at the preparatory commission, the secretary, Fr Bugnini, was truly the architect of the reforms that were about to begin. He organized and coordinated the work of the groups of

---

21. Bugnini, *Reform*, 944–50.
22. For the general plan see ibid., 63–65. These study groups are often referred to by the Latin term that was used for them: *Coetus*.

consultors. While he did not actually preside over the plenary sessions, he did establish their agendas[23] and transmitted the texts to be examined to the members. Also, he had far greater and easier access to the pope than did the cardinal president of the *Consilium*. To show that the liturgical reform was conducted in close collaboration with Paul VI, Bugnini later specified:

> How many evenings I spent with him studying the many and often lengthy files heaped on his table! He read and reflected on them all, line by line, word by word, annotating everything in black, red, and blue pencil and criticizing it if need be with a logical mind that could formulate ten questions on a single point.[24]

This description applies especially to the years 1968–1969, however, after Lercaro's departure and during the most intense phase of the preparation of the new *Ordo Missae*.

Neither the members nor the consultors of the *Consilium* resided in Rome permanently for the entire duration of the reform's elaboration. Each group had a *relator* (spokesman) in charge of liaising with the geographically dispersed other members and of drawing up a report for examination at the *Consilium*'s general meetings. After that, *schemas* were drawn up and examined. Piero Marini has established a list of those drawn up at Bugnini's initiative.[25] From March 1964 to July 1975, 439 *schemas* were examined and ultimately resulted in the composition and promulgation of the new rites and liturgical books.

After two preliminary meetings (January 15 and February 15, 1964), the *Consilium* started holding ordinary assemblies (*Ordinaria*) that gathered the members present in Rome as well as some consultors. They were to have taken place every other Thursday, but there were only ever two ordinary assemblies (March 20 and April 13, 1964), as such a rhythm seemed too rigid for the multiple *schemas*

---

23. Cardinal Lercaro "left the discussion topics and agendas up to Msgr Bugnini": Martimort, "Cardinal G. Lercaro," 386.

24. Bugnini, *Reform*, xxviii.

25. Piero Marini, "Elenco degli 'schemata' del 'Consilium' e della Congregazione per il culto divino," *Notitiae* 17 (October–November 1982): 453–772. P. Marini was Archbishop Bugnini's secretary, 1965–1975.

that were being launched all at the same time and for the multiple cases and requests presented to the *Consilium*. Only plenary sessions (*plenaria*) took place, usually over the course of several days. Meanwhile, Fr Bugnini would coordinate the study groups' work and had texts and answers drawn up.

The *Consilium* had eleven plenary sessions from March 1964 to October 1968. After the creation of the Congregation for Divine Worship (May 8, 1969), there followed a twelfth and last session (November 1969) and then, from 1970 on, plenary assemblies took place within the new Congregation.

Dom Botte, who, as a consultor and *relator* on the *Consilium*, was in charge of the reform of the first part of the Pontifical, has described the manner in which the plenary sessions were carried out.[26] They took place in two sessions. First, usually over several days, the consultors gathered:

> In the former [session] each relator was invited in turn to submit the results of his group's work to the full body of consultors present. Since the latter's feedback was to be based on a written text, the relator was supposed to send to the secretariat beforehand a report which was copied and supplied to all the consultors.... [He] read his report line by line and responded to the questions and objections raised. All could speak and propose corrections. A discussion ensued, and attempts were made to find a solution which satisfied the majority.

Then followed the meeting of the members (cardinals and bishops) who alone had a deliberative voice. The consultors were again present and could ask to take the floor, but only the members could vote on the texts that had been presented and discussed:

> The relator again read his report as it was revised by the observations and corrections proposed by the consultors. When the discussion could not reach an agreement, recourse was had to a vote. Most of the time it was by a show of hands. In more serious cases the voting was in secret.... After a draft had been examined part-by-part in this way, the full text was considered as a whole, and the

---

26. Botte, *From Silence to Participation*, 126.

final vote of the commission [*Consilium*] was considered definitive. The draft would then be submitted for the pope's approval.

It may be added that, at Fr Bugnini's initiative, the *Consilium* was
adept at broadcasting its work and the spirit that reigned over it.
Immediately after the March 1964 meeting, a circular letter was sent
to all the apostolic nuncios in the world asking them to relay to
bishops and bishops' conferences instructions on the implementation of the liturgical reform.[27] The following October, the presidents of national liturgical commissions who had come to Rome
were invited to the *Consilium* to receive information, advice, and
directives. Then, sometime later, liturgical book publishers and
directors of liturgical journals from the world over were invited.[28]
Fr Bugnini embodied a perfect mix of know-how and communication skills.

Concelebration and Communion Under Both Kinds

The first two *schemas* prepared by the *Consilium* and examined in
the earliest days (April 15, 1964) were those dealing with concelebration and communion under both kinds. Until then, both had been
used in a very limited way and under precise circumstances in the
Latin Church.

The extension of concelebration had been requested periodically
by certain liturgists and bishops since the 1950s. This had occasioned discussions and decisions under Pius XII. The preparatory
commission and then the Council's Constitution, as we have seen,
asked "to extend permission for concelebration" in five "cases" and
for a new rite of concelebration to be drawn up (*SC* 57–58).

As for communion under both kinds, which had progressively
fallen into disuse,[29] it had been demanded by the Hussites in the
fourteenth century (to the point of precipitating a civil war), then

27. Marini, 47–48.
28. Ibid., 89–90.
29. At the end of the thirteenth century, Saint Thomas Aquinas reports that "it
is the custom of many churches for the body of Christ to be given to the communi-
cant without His blood," *Summa theologiae* III.80.12.

by Luther who had denounced "refusing the chalice to the faithful" as one of the marks of the "Babylonian captivity of the Church." According to Luther, Jesus "says, not by way of permission, but of command: 'Drink of it, all of you' (Mt 26:27)" and "the two kinds constitute one complete sacrament, which may not be divided."[30] Against Hus and Luther, the Council of Trent had reaffirmed "that Christ whole and entire and a true sacrament is received even under either species alone."

That Vatican II granted communion under both species to the faithful under certain circumstances is therefore somewhat unexpected. It provides three examples of such circumstances: "to the newly ordained in the Mass of their sacred ordination, to the newly professed in the Mass of their religious profession, and to the newly baptized in the Mass which follows their baptism" (SC 55).

Consequently, the *Consilium* drew up two new rites for concelebration and for communion under both kinds. Study group 16 was in charge of the work. Its relator was Dom Vagaggini and its secretary was another Benedictine, Dom Franquesa of the abbey in Montserrat. Use was also made of the work of the conciliar preparatory commission; the relator of the subcommission *De Concelebratione Sacramenti* at the time had been Dom Capelle, who died in 1961.

Several successive drafts were drawn up; the *Consilium* authorized more and more "experiments" before adopting the final rite. This was to be the practice for other texts too. By collating different sources, one can make out the steps that this process took over a little more than a year (November 1963–March 1965):[31]

- November 1963 (therefore even before the official creation of the *Consilium*): a first draft on concelebration, by Dom Cipriano Vagaggini, OSB.

---

30. Martin Luther, *The Babylonian Captivity of the Church*, trans. A. T. W. Steinhäuser in *Martin Luther, Three Treatises* (Philadelphia: Fortress Press, 1970), 135–36.

31. *Il Cardinale Lercaro 50°. Genova–Bologna* (Bologna: Casa della carità, 1964); *L'Osservatore Romano*, 26 March 1965; Bugnini, *Reform*, 72, 124–34; Martimort, "Le cardinal Lercaro," 386; Guillaume Derville, *La concélébration eucharistique. Du symbolisme à la réalité* (Montreal: Wilson & Lafleur, 2011).

• April 2, 1964: the first draft is sent to roughly thirty consultors in different countries.

• April 14–20, 1964: the revised draft is examined during the *Consilium*'s second plenary session.

• May 17, 1964: with special permission from Paul VI, Cardinal Lercaro, on the occasion of his priestly Jubilee, celebrates Mass with other priests in Bologna. This was the first experimental concelebration. It was filmed.

• June 18–20, 1964: a third version of the draft is examined during the *Consilium*'s third plenary session. On June 18 the film of the concelebration in Bologna was shown to the members and consultors in attendance.

• June 20, 1964: the fourth version of the draft is presented to Paul VI.

• June 26, 1964: the pope authorizes experimental celebrations of the new rite of concelebration in six Benedictine abbeys (San Anselmo in Rome, Montserrat, En-Calcat, Maredsous, Maria Laach, and Collegeville) and at Le Saulchoir, the Dominican convent in Paris.

• July 3, 1964: the pope authorizes the *Consilium* to deliver indults for concelebration and communion under both species "in particular cases." These are no longer "experiments" but the concession of rites that have yet to be formalized.

• September 14, 1964: the pope concelebrates the opening Mass of the third session of the Council (he would also concelebrate the closing Mass of this session).

• December 10, 1964: the fifth draft is prepared after examination of the proposals sent in by the communities that had "experimented" with concelebration.

• January 20, 1965: the final text (sixth draft) is presented to the pope.

• February 25, 1965: Paul VI concelebrates with twenty-four newly created cardinals; a huge square altar is built for the circumstance.[32]

• March 7, 1965: the decree *Ecclesiae Semper* for the publication of the *Ritus servandus in concelebratione Missae* is promulgated for implementation on Holy Thursday, April 15.

---

32. Photograph published on the front page of *L'Osservatore Romano*, 26 March 1965.

The Benedictine abbeys chosen to "experiment" with concelebration had been picked because one of their monks was among the consultors or experts at the *Consilium*. It was they who presided over or organized the experimental concelebrations in their abbeys. So, for example, Dom Adalbert Franquesa, secretary of the group that had drawn up the draft on concelebration, directed the ceremonies at the abbey of Montserrat. In July 1964, Fr Bugnini wrote to him: "How are the 'experimenta' going?," adding: "I'll be pleased if Montserrat would put together a nice album for the Holy See."[33] Indeed the abbeys and the Dominican convent where these experimental concelebrations were conducted—they each performed several—had to send a report to the *Consilium* and, if possible, take photographs of the ceremonies. These were then shown to the pope.

At the very same time that these *experimenta* were underway, the *Consilium* was granting authorizations for concelebration to all takers. Between July 3, 1964 and March 1965, 720 indults for concelebration had been granted to bishops and diocesan priests and 206 indults to religious families. In all, "over 1,500 concelebrations" had taken place, according to Bugnini's account. It is fair to say that concelebration had become familiar to a great number of the faithful and communities before the rite was ever formalized.

There is no need to go into the details of the decree, which simply gives a long doctrinal exposition of the theological basis for this practice. The *Rite of Concelebration* that the Consilium published on the same date (March 7, 1965) outlines five instances when such a concelebration may occur: "both the chrism Mass and the evening Mass on Holy Thursday"; in councils and synods; at the blessing of an Abbot; at the conventual Mass and the principal Mass in parishes "when the needs of the faithful do not require that all priests available celebrate individually"; at priests' meetings.[34]

---

33. Fr Bugnini to Dom A. Franquesa, 27 July 1964, Montserrat Abbey Archives.

34. Sacred Congregation of Rites/Consilium, Decree *Ecclesiae Semper, AAS* 57 (1965): 410–12, *DOL* 222; id., *Rite of Concelebration* (Vatican: Polyglot Press, 1965), 13, *DOL* 223.1794.

There were variations regarding the number of concelebrants, their position relative to the altar, and the liturgical vestments they were to wear. The *Consilium*'s first drafts indicated fifty as a maximum. Paul VI had wanted a maximum of twenty or twenty-five concelebrants, all of them standing around the altar (as had been done on February 25, 1965) and all vested in the same liturgical vestments. Yet Bugnini, in his presentation of the rite, specified that "it is not necessary that all touch the altar materially"[35] and the 1967 Instruction on the liturgy, on which more later, would restrict the sacred vestments to the principal celebrant alone while the other celebrants might vest in only alb and stole.

On the very day that the rite of concelebration was published, March 7, 1965, the *Ritus communionis sub utraque specie* ("Rite of Communion under Both Kinds") was published too. The conciliar Constitution had granted this practice of communion, specifying that it could be reintroduced "in instances to be specified by the Apostolic See . . . at the discretion of the bishops" (*SC* 55). Yet a specialist on this question, Sulpician Father Charles Michel-Jean, who had been one of the experts consulted for the preparation of this rite, was later to acknowledge that there was no doctrinal reason to reintroduce communion under both kinds: "To tell the truth, the faithful and the clergy did not call for the restoration of this rite all that much. If the Church has now undertaken this restoration, it is from a positive desire on her part to bring out a forgotten but important value."

This restoration was symbolically important ("the restoration of communion at the chalice must be understood within the framework of a liturgical reform that seeks above all to give back to sacred signs the fullness of their signifying power") and also an ecumenical aim (the Orthodox and the Protestants practice communion from the chalice).[36] The Council had given three "examples" of communion under both species: "to the ordained at the Mass of their ordina-

---

35. *L'Osservatore Romano,* 26 March 1965.

36. Charles Michel-Jean, "La Communion au calice," *La Maison-Dieu* 85 (1966): 168–78 at 173–74.

tion, to the professed at the Mass of their religious profession, to the newly baptized at the Mass following their baptism" (*SC* 55).

The March 7 decree extended this possibility to eleven cases and indicated four manners of communion under both species: by drinking straight from the chalice; by intinction (the host is dipped in the chalice); with a *calamus* (also called tube or fistula); with a spoon.

In practice, the first two manners of receiving the consecrated wine at communion prevailed. Note also that in the Instruction *Eucharisticum Mysterium* (1967), communion from the chalice was extended to other circumstances, particularly for groups on a spiritual retreat.[37]

In his presentation of these two rites published in *L'Osservatore Romano*, Fr Bugnini considered them as "two pearls of the liturgical renewal . . . two rites, so desired and so beloved, that have garnered interest everywhere." With historical hindsight, one realizes that while concelebration has become generalized far beyond what the texts quoted above foresaw (which has given rise to doctrinal discussions), communion from the chalice has remained an "exceptional practice" to this day. This is what historian Dominique Belœil has noted, adding:

> Its place in the liturgical reform is marginal if compared to the great reforms of the Mass in French, the place of the Word of God, the laity's role in the celebrations, or even concelebration. The absence of demand among the faithful, if not a certain reticence that can easily be verified in religious communities where communion under both kinds is possible every Sunday, is noteworthy.[38]

---

37. Instruction *Eucharisticum Mysterium*, 25 May 1967, DOL 179.1261.

38. Dominique Belœil, "Le Vin au calice depuis le concile Vatican II après plusieurs siècles de disparition," in H. Cahuzac and M. Joly eds., *Le Corps, le vin et les images* (Paris: L'Harmattan, 2005), 96. [These comments do not necessarily reflect the situation outside of France. For example, in the United States of America, communion under both kinds in the Ordinary Form is ubiquitous and often treated as indispensable, even for daily Mass.—*Trans.*]

The Instruction *Inter Oecumenici* and the 1965 *Ordo Missae*

The decree on concelebration and communion under both kinds is dated March 7, 1965. On the same day the important Instruction *Inter Oecumenici* and the new rite of Mass issuing from it took effect. This Instruction "on the orderly carrying out of the Constitution on the Liturgy," dated September 26, 1964, was presented in its French edition as

> the major document of the first step of the reform [in which] what is immediately possible without having to wait for the liturgical books to be recast systematically, which will take years of work, has been decided. . . . The Instruction ensures the transition between the preconciliar liturgy and the deeper restoration; it is not an ad hoc adaptation, but a step along the way.[39]

The text was explicitly presented as having been "prepared" by the *Consilium*, but it was signed both by Cardinal Lercaro, its president, and by Cardinal Larraona, prefect of the Congregation of Rites.[40] Although its object was the same as that of the motu proprio *Sacram Liturgiam* of January 1965, the Instruction was far more detailed. Certain points were taken over nearly verbatim while others had not been mentioned in the motu proprio at all.

The Instruction was organized in five chapters and included ninety-nine articles. It followed the order of the conciliar Constitution and a great many of its articles, though not all, explicitly refer to the conciliar text. It authorized or mandated "that those measures that are practicable before revision of the liturgical books go into effect immediately." Above all, and unlike the motu proprio, it had an entire article dealing with reforms in the *Ordo* of the Mass.

Though not yet amounting to a complete overhaul of the *Ordo*, the Instruction outlined in twelve articles those changes that were to take place in the meantime, notably including:

- the recitation of the *Pater Noster* in the vernacular by priest and faithful together;

---

39. *La Réforme liturgique. Décisions et directives d'application* (Paris: Centurion, 1964), 8–9.
40. *L'Osservatore Romano*, 18 October 1964; for the English version see *DOL* 23.

• two unexplained suppressions: "The last Gospel is omitted; the Leonine Prayers are suppressed";
• the introduction before the Offertory of a "universal prayer or prayer of the faithful" (the common expression was to become "prayer of the faithful");
• the authorization of the vernacular language for the readings (Epistle and Gospel) and for the chants of the Ordinary of the Mass (the *Kyrie, Gloria, Credo, Sanctus-Benedictus,* and *Agnus Dei*).

Without getting into the detail of all ninety-nine articles of this Instruction, note the ninety-first, which introduces the possibility of celebrating Mass "facing the people": "The main altar should preferably be freestanding, to permit walking around it and celebration facing the people. Its location in the place of worship should be truly central so that the attention of the whole congregation naturally focuses on it." This possibility of Mass "facing the people" was given with no reference to the conciliar Constitution because such a possibility is not to be found in it. Yet this concession was soon to become the norm, the pope himself giving the example.

The September 26, 1964 Instruction was presented as coming into force on March 7, 1965, the first Sunday in Lent. In January 1965, a new *Ordo Missae* in keeping with these new norms was published by the Vatican Polyglot Press, along with a new *Ritus servandus*. Both of these, much rather than the Instruction, gave the Mass a new configuration.

On January 29, Fr Bugnini presented it in a long article published in *L'Osservatore Romano*.[41] In it he insisted on the fact that despite his article's title ("The New *Ordo Missae*"), "it ought to be called *renewed, updated,* for, despite its touchups, adaptations, and corrections, the *Ordo Missae* has not changed its appearance substantially." He added that the adaptation was done according to two "imperatives": the distinction between the "liturgy of the Word" and the "liturgy of the Eucharist," and the "devout, active, and conscious participation of the faithful."

Fr Bugnini insisted on the fact that the Canon had not been modified and still had to be said by the priest in a low voice ("the rubrics

41. Bugnini, "Il nuovo Ordo Missae," *L'Osservatore Romano,* 29 January 1965.

and the formulas of the Eucharistic Prayer remain unchanged"). But he also used blunt expressions: "The Gospel is reserved to the celebrant, or to the deacon in sung Masses. The latter incenses the Book of Gospels, but from now on he will skip the censing of the celebrant, which is a rather recent and out-of-place ceremony."

Regarding the use of "the people's language" that was now to become the language of most of the Mass, Fr Bugnini acknowledged practical difficulties due to the fact that definitive translations were not yet ready in every language or approved by the Holy See. He granted that there would be a time of uncertainty:

> The lack of time and sometimes the lack of technical means and personnel have added to the difficulties. Be that as it may, even if they are not perfect, translations are in force or will be. Experience, time, and use will allow the texts to be polished and perfected in the years to come so that they may garner the greatest possible approval and worthily express the Church's prayer.

Paul VI, as a way of lending authority to this vast liturgical reform on the day when the new *Ordo Missae* came into force on March 7, 1965, celebrated Mass at All Saints' church in Rome. The Mass, for the first time, was celebrated in Italian (only the Canon was in Latin) and facing the people; the altar stood on a wooden stage built in the church's sanctuary for the occasion. In the allocution he gave a few hours later for the Angelus on Saint Peter's Square, the pope justified "the sacrifice of centuries-old traditions" that had just taken place:

> Today is a memorable Sunday in the spiritual history of the Church: the vernacular, as you have perceived this morning, has officially taken its place within liturgical worship. The Church has judged this measure—raised and debated at the Council—to be necessary to make its prayer understandable and grasped by all. The good of the faithful calls for this kind of action, making possible their active share in the Church's public worship. The Church has sacrificed its native tongue, Latin, a language that is sacred, measured, beautiful, richly expressive, and graceful. The Church has made the sacrifice of an age-old tradition and above all of unity in language among diverse peoples to bow to a higher universality, and outreach to all peoples.

Paul VI was convinced that the faithful would "pass over from being simply spectators to becoming active participants."[42]

"Reactions" and "Fanciful Initiatives"

Paul VI had explained that the Church had made a "sacrifice" in giving up Latin, but that she had done so for the good of the faithful. Within a few days of the implementation of the liturgical reform Cardinal Lercaro had used the same argument. He had published a long article in the high-volume Catholic daily *l'Avennire d'Italia*. The article dealt both with "negative reactions" against the reform and with "deplorable" initiatives.[43]

The *Consilium* president had in the first instance deplored the "negative reactions...of persons and circles who consider the reform to be harmful to the Church and to souls, are reluctant towards it, or accept it begrudgingly and without conviction."

Cardinal Lercaro explained these reactions by a "doctrinal insufficiency, a phenomenon of ignorance" and by "the force of tradition (not however of authentic tradition, which maintains the spirit of institutions, but of shortsighted tradition) and the force of habit, 'routine', which all of us know how hard it is to get rid of."

The cardinal devoted a long part of his argument to showing that "Latin has not been completely eliminated from the liturgy,"[44] just as sacred music, particularly Gregorian chant, had not been completely eliminated.

The association *Una Voce* was born at this time. It drew its origin from a work by Bernadette Lécureux, *Le Latin, langue de l'Église* (1964). This book had defended the preeminence of Latin as a liturgical language in four arguments: it is a "fixed ... sacred ... universal" language and the "traditional language of the Church." Following the book's success, Bernadette Lécureux and her husband,

---

42. Paul VI, Remarks at the Angelus, 7 March 1965, *L'Osservatore Romano*, 8–9 March 1965; English translation, *DOL* 26.

43. Lercaro, *l'Avennire d'Italia*, 2 March 1965.

44. The president of the *Consilium* claimed that "the Divine Office, which is more especially the priest's and monk's prayer, remains entirely in Latin," which was already no longer true, even according to the official texts.

Georges Cerbelaud-Salagnac, created the association *Una Voce* in Paris early in 1965. Its goal was "the preservation and development of the Latin liturgy, of Gregorian chant, and of sacred art in the Catholic liturgy." The association soon flourished and expanded into other countries; in 1966 the International Federation *Una Voce* was created. It was to be very active in its dealings with the Holy See in the wake of the liturgical reform.

Cardinal Lercaro, while he did not mention any group explicitly, judged that no unilateral and unconditional attachment to Latin and to Gregorian chant was justified any longer, on the grounds that "the historical period that we call Tridentine is closed." The "new imperatives of new times" required "sacrifices," one of which was that of the omnipresence of Latin in the liturgy.

The president of the *Consilium* then went on to the inverse "reaction," that which, while welcoming the reforms introduced into the liturgy, "tends to go too far, to supplant the authority of the Church and, in a certain way, to force her hand." Cardinal Lercaro gave concrete examples of "fanciful," "deplorable" initiatives taken by "individuals and groups—with excellent intentions, to be sure, but not without pretension": "Throughout the world, we have seen some recite the entire Canon out loud, others recite it with the people in the local language. Elsewhere, communion is distributed by placing the host in the open hands of the faithful, etc." As an aside, note that this last practice, deemed "fanciful" in 1965, was soon to be authorized far and wide, as we shall see.

Mysterium Fidei

Besides aberrant or "fanciful" liturgical practices, there was a proliferation of writings (books and articles) in which theologians outlined new conceptions of the Eucharist. Paul VI found it necessary to intervene solemnly in an encyclical, *Mysterium Fidei*, published on September 3, 1965.[45] In this encyclical "on the doctrine and worship of the Eucharist," the pope expressed his "concern and anxiety" about "opinions that upset the faithful and fill their minds with

---

45. *AAS* 57 (1965): 753–74; *DOL* 176.

great confusion about matters of faith." He vigorously condemned the theory according to which "the Mass 'of the community'" had greater value than the so-called private Mass, since "every Mass, even though a priest may offer it in private, is not a private matter; it is an act of Christ and of the Church."

The pope also called into question the replacement of the doctrine of "transubstantiation" with notions of "'transignification' or 'transfinalization." Moreover, Paul VI protested against the opinion that "Christ the Lord is no longer present in the consecrated hosts left after the celebration of the sacrifice of the Mass is ended."

On all these points, the pope was reaffirming the traditional doctrine by relying on the definitions of earlier councils and providing abundant texts quoted from the Fathers of the Church. He stressed the importance of doctrinal formulas and of theological notions relating to the mystery of the Eucharist:

> We must religiously respect the rule of terminology; after centuries of effort and under the protection of the Holy Spirit the Church has established it and confirmed it by the authority of councils; that norm often became the watchword and the banner of orthodox belief. Let no one arbitrarily or under the pretext of new science presume to change it. Would we allow the dogmatic formulas of the ecumenical councils concerning the mysteries of the most blessed Trinity and the Incarnation to be declared unsuited to our contemporaries and other formulas to be rashly substituted? In like manner, we must not put up with anyone's personal wish to modify the formulas in which the Council of Trent set forth the mystery of the Eucharist for belief.

Paul VI also encouraged the faithful to attend Mass daily, if possible, to receive frequent communion, and not to neglect visits to the Blessed Sacrament.

This reaffirmation of the traditional doctrine on the Mass as sacrifice and on the Real Presence in the Eucharist through transubstantiation was necessary because of the doctrinal deviations proliferating in several countries. It was also necessary because the transformations that the liturgy was undergoing at the time were causing confusion. Paul VI therefore intervened to issue a warning to some and to reassure others.

The Torn Tunic

The Mass that Paul VI had said in Italian and facing the people in March 1965 had attracted considerable attention. Many churches in several countries had not waited for this papal example to put into practice (with varying degrees of anarchy) the changes that had been announced. During the *Consilium*'s seventh plenary session, Paul VI received all of its participants, both members and consultors, on October 13, 1966, and delivered a significant address.[46] While expressing his great satisfaction with the work already accomplished, he gave recommendations for the ongoing general reform. He asked those working at it to have

> certain qualities of spirit. One is a reverence for the sacred that prompts us to honor the ceremonies used by the Church in worshiping God. Another is respect for tradition, which has passed on a priceless heritage worthy of veneration. Necessary as well is a sense of history, which has bearing on the way the rites under revision were formed, on their genuine meaning, either as prayer or as symbol. . . .

These pressing recommendations ("the search must be for what is best rather than for what is new") were accompanied with a request that might have seemed like a reproach. Indeed, Paul VI wanted the *Consilium* to exert its "guidance of the broad and multiform reform efforts" in the liturgy worldwide with greater "vigilance" and "prudence":

> Your own Consilium has a responsibility of vigilance during this period when new forms of divine worship are being tested and introduced in the different regions of the Church. You must check misguided attempts that may here and there appear and constrain those who follow their own preferences at the risk of disturbing the right order of public prayer and of occasioning doctrinal errors.

Soon the *Consilium* would be taken to task in a book that came out as the first manifesto of resistance to the liturgical renewal: *La*

---

46. *DOL* 84.

Tunica stracciata. Lettera di un cattolico sulla "Riforma liturgica."[47] Its author was a well-known Italian writer, Tito Casini.

As a preamble, he explained that he had written his book by the summer of 1965, after Paul VI celebrated his famous Italian Mass in a Roman parish. He then hesitated to publish it after the pope, in his Apostolic Letter *Sacrificium Laudis,* had solemnly exhorted the superiors general of religious orders to keep Latin and Gregorian chant.[48] Then, as liturgical upheaval continued in Italian parishes, Tito Casini resolved to publish his book to defend "the Catholic liturgy [which] continued to be attacked—and is still being attacked—in its forms, language and song."

His work, which is at once polemical and superbly written, presented itself as an open letter to an unnamed cardinal whom everyone identified as Cardinal Lercaro, president of the *Consilium,* here qualified as a "Luther redivivus." The book caused a fracas that was magnified by its being prefaced by another cardinal, Cardinal Bacci, onetime secretary of Briefs to Princes and an eminent Latinist. This was no courtesy preface; it was a four-page-long text. Cardinal Bacci explained: "I consider Tito Casini, whom I have known since boyhood, one of the foremost Catholic writers of Italy. His style—fresh, frank and caustic—is like a gust of pure mountain air." He also stated that "if what he has here set down may seem to some too little reverent, all will be bound to admit it was dictated solely by his passionate love for the Church, and her liturgical decorum."

Cardinal Bacci judged that the liturgical reform as it was being applied was a betrayal of the Council, which stated that "particular law remaining in force, the use of the Latin language is to be preserved in the Latin rites" (*SC* 36.1). In concrete terms, Cardinal Bacci asked

> at least in cathedral churches, sanctuaries and tourist centers, and everywhere that enough priests are to be found, for a certain number of Latin Masses to be celebrated, at fixed times, to meet the just desires of all, whatever their nationality, who prefer Latin to

47. Published in Florence in April 1967. English translation: *The Torn Tunic. Letter of a Catholic on the "Liturgical Reform"* (Rome: Fidelity Books, 1967).
48. Dated August 15, 1966; *DOL* 421.

the vernacular, and Gregorian chant to the mean and trivial type of popular ditty that is today attempting to oust it.

Tito Casini's work came out in the Spring of 1967, a few days before the *Consilium*'s eighth plenary session, which took place April 10–19. The Italian press took hold of the polemic and published a great deal of articles quoting Casini's criticisms and the support Cardinal Bacci had lent him. As soon as he had had a chance to read the book, Cardinal Lercaro realized the intensity of the attacks and was hurt by his confrere's preface. Cardinal Bacci had stigmatized "frenzied and fanatical innovators" without distinguishing *Consilium* authorities and parish-based initiatives.

On April 5 Cardinal Lercaro addressed a letter to Cardinal Tisserant, dean of the Sacred College, to Cardinal Cicognani, Secretary of State, and to Archbishop Dell'Acqua, substitute at the Secretariat of State.[49] He asked that "a public and concrete reparation" be made to him and to the *Consilium* via an article published in *L'Osservatore Romano*.[50] Ten days later, not having received an answer and having fruitlessly attempted to gain an audience with the pope, Lercaro left Rome on the evening of April 15 and went back to his diocese of Bologna; he left the *Consilium* to pursue its work without him.

Fr Bugnini addressed a telegram to the pope in the *Consilium*'s name to protest the criticisms that had been made against Cardinal Lercaro and the liturgical reform. Paul VI did not respond to this telegram directly. At first, he simply had his Secretary of State send a message to Cardinal Lercaro. Cardinal Cicognani transmitted the Apostolic Blessing to the *Consilium* and to its president.[51] Finally, on April 17, Cardinal Lercaro returned to Rome to resume presidency of the *Consilium*, where he was given a comforting welcome.

Two days later, April 19, Paul VI received the members and consultors of the *Consilium* and gave a long speech in which he renewed his trust in the organization and defended its president. He denounced an "unjust and irreverent attack" and wished to "express

---

49. Nazari Sauro Onofri, *Le Due anime del cardinal Lercaro* (Bologna: Capelli, 1987), 169.
50. Bugnini, *Reform*, 164–65.
51. Telegram published in *L'Osservatore Romano*, 16 April 1967.

to Cardinal Lercaro [his] regret and [his] support." The pope also refuted Casini's accusations. Paul VI stated:

> Obviously, we do not agree with this publication, which surely in no one inspires piety nor helps the cause it pretends to advance, namely, that of preserving the Latin language in the liturgy. Latin is an issue certainly deserving serious attention, but the issue cannot be solved in a way that is opposed to the great principle confirmed by the Council, namely, that liturgical prayer, accommodated to the understanding of the people, is to be intelligible. Nor can it be solved in opposition to another principle called for by the collectivity of human culture, namely, that peoples' deepest and sincerest sentiments can best be expressed through the vernacular as it is in actual usage.[52]

In the same address Paul VI voiced his indignation against the "disciplinary irregularity" that was spreading in the liturgy, forms "deliberately patterned on the personal preference of certain individuals and often ... wholly at odds with the precepts now in force in the Church," "upsetting examples," a "widening movement toward a liturgy ... rashly described as 'desacralized.'"

Paul VI asked the bishops to "keep a close watch on such episodes and [to] safeguard the balance proper to Catholic worship in the liturgical and religious domain." He also asked priests and faithful not to "allow themselves to burn with the inane desire for experiments inspired by private preference." Just as he had done a year earlier, he urged the *Consilium* to "control wisely the specific liturgical experiments that seem worth bringing to fruition in a responsible and considered way."

The Second Instruction on the Liturgical Reform (May 1967)

Two weeks after the *Consilium's* eighth plenary session, the second Instruction on the reform was published.[53] Like the first one (September 1964) it was cosigned by the president of the Consilium,

---

52. Paul VI, Address to the members and *periti* of the Consilium, April 19, 1967; English translation *DOL* 86.
53. Instruction *Tres abhinc annos*, dated May 4, 1967; *DOL* 39.

Cardinal Lercaro, and the prefect of the Congregation of Rites, Cardinal Larraona. This Instruction, again with a view to encouraging the "participation of the faithful in the liturgy"—the expression recurs several times throughout the document—and "to make the liturgical rites, especially the Mass, clearer and better and better understood," introduced significant modifications to the celebration of Mass. On the one hand it continued to simplify the rite of the Mass by reducing the number of the priest's genuflections (n. 7) and the number of kisses given to the altar (n. 8), and by retaining only one sign of the cross over the offerings (n. 11). On the other hand, the Instruction completed the introduction of the vernacular into the Mass by allowing the Canon to be said aloud (n. 10) and in the vernacular (n. 28).

Fr Bugnini presented these changes and commented on them in a long article published in *L'Osservatore Romano* on the very day of the Instruction's publication.[54] He justified the simplifications by minimizing their importance; he did not consider that they might contribute to any further desacralization of the Mass: "These modifications are not important." Fr Bugnini was also somewhat nonchalant when speaking of the genuflections and signs of the cross: "The celebration in the language of the people is often done facing the assembly; this makes certain gestures seem anachronistic or superfluous ... which, especially in certain circles, causes incomprehension and weariness."

He also announced that a new "ordering of the Mass" would be presented at the next Synod.

This announcement, as well as the modifications the second Instruction had just introduced, worried those who were attached to the traditional form of the liturgy. A few weeks after this document's publication, the International Federation *Una Voce*, with Eric de Saventhem as its president, addressed a long supplication to Paul VI on May 25 to express his "consternation and stupefaction."[55] The federation Una Voce was afraid that the new reforms might

---

54. *L'Osservatore Romano*, 7 May 1967.
55. Saventhem to Paul VI, 25 May 1967, published in *Una Voce* 14 (May–June–July 1967): 2–4.

contribute to fostering the "weakening of the faith" and drive some of the faithful away from church.[56] Like Cardinal Bacci a month earlier, it asked "that the ancient Roman liturgy, that is, the religious rite in Latin with its own chant, Gregorian chant, should continue to be celebrated side by side with that in the vernacular in all the Catholic churches of the world."

56. In 1976 Georges Brassens, a popular French folk singer, famously sang "Sans le latin, la messe nous emmerde…" [a vulgar expression, roughly "Mass stinks without Latin"].

8

The "New Mass"

T HE INCREMENTAL REFORMS brought about by the September 1964 and May 1967 Instructions opened the way to a general reform of the Mass. They lay the groundwork for it in two transitional phases, as it were.

A completely new rite of the Mass was slated for preparation from the very beginning of the *Consilium*. During the fifth plenary session in April 1965 (20 members and 41 experts were in attendance), the possibility of modifying the Canon of the Mass was brought up. As Archbishop Bugnini himself was later to admit, however, a very broad majority of members and consultors was of the opinion that this "venerable document" was not to be touched.

The first complete draft of a new *Ordo Missae* was ready for the sixth plenary session (October 18–26, 1965). Msgr Wagner, the relator for the tenth group, presented it. It was the occasion for two "experimentations" that took place in the chapel of the "Maria Bambina" Institute: the first in Italian on October 20, the second in French on October 22. The two celebrations of this "normative" Mass, as it was called, took place behind closed doors in the presence of *Consilium* members, who were then able to share their impressions in one of the Institute's meeting rooms.[1] Paul VI had some concerns regarding this reform of the *Ordo Missae*. On three different occasions (October 25, 1965, December 10, 1965, and March 7, 1966), he had his Secretary of State, Cardinal Cicognani, address official letters to Cardinal Lercaro to recommend prudence and reserving to the Holy See any decision involving "any possible

---

1. Bugnini, *Reform*, 151–52, 342–46.

changes proposed for the rite of celebration of the divine sacrifice."[2]

On June 20, 1966, the revised first draft of the new Mass was presented to Paul VI by Cardinal Lercaro. The pope wanted two important changes:

> • the present anaphora [the Roman Canon] is to be left untouched; two or three other anaphoras should be composed, or sought in existing texts, that could be used during certain defined seasons.
> • the *Kyrie* should be retained when the *Gloria* is not said; when the liturgy prescribes the *Gloria*, however, the *Kyrie* should be replaced with another penitential prayer.[3]

Consequently, a *Consilium* subcommission prepared three new anaphoras (or Eucharistic Prayers). Two were new compositions while the third (which became the second Eucharistic Prayer in the new *Ordo Missae*) was inspired by the anaphora of Saint Hippolytus.[†]

Archbishop Bugnini was later to acknowledge that one of these new Eucharistic Prayers (which became the fourth Eucharistic Prayer) was put together in haste, "a kind of forced labor."[4] A consultor on that subcommission, Fr Bouyer, gave the same description (not without humor and irony) for the composition of the second Eucharistic Prayer that he prepared with Dom Botte, the famous Hippolytus specialist. He had to compose it posthaste, within a twenty-four-hour period:

> Between the indiscriminately archeologizing fanatics who wanted to banish the *Sanctus* and the intercessions from the Eucharistic Prayer by taking Hippolytus's Eucharist as is, and those others who couldn't have cared less about his alleged *Apostolic Tradition* and wanted a slapdash Mass, Dom Botte and I were commissioned to patch up its text with a view to inserting these elements, which are certainly quite ancient—by the next morning! Luckily, I discov-

---

2. Letters published ibid., 152, n. 30.

3. Ibid., 163, 346.

† The authenticity of the anaphora of Saint Hippolytus and its relevance to the Roman tradition is no longer a matter of scholarly consensus.—*Ed.*

4. Ibid., 163.

ered, if not in a text by Hippolytus himself certainly in one in his style, a felicitous formula on the Holy Ghost that could provide a transition of the *Vere Sanctus* type to the short epiclesis. For his part Botte produced an intercession worthier of Paul Reboux's "In the manner of…" than of his actual scholarship. Still, I cannot reread that improbable composition without recalling the Trastevere café terrace where we had to put the finishing touches to our assignment in order to show up with it at the Bronze Gate by the time our masters had set![5]

Nine new Prefaces were composed at this time, of which eight were retained. Fr Bouyer sees them in a more positive light: "The only element undeserving of criticism in this new missal was the enrichment it received, thanks particularly to the restoration of a good number of splendid prefaces taken over from ancient sacramentaries. . . ."[6]

An Experimental Mass at the Synod of 1967

The new Mass in its completed structure was presented to some 180 cardinals and bishops in a Synod at the Vatican in 1967. This first postconciliar Synod was to deal with several topics: the revision of the code of canon law, doctrinal questions, and the liturgical reform.

On October 21, Cardinal Lercaro presented the assembled cardinals and bishops with a report describing the new structure of the Mass and the changes introduced into it, as well as the reform of the Divine Office. On October 24, Fr Bugnini celebrated a "normative" Mass before the Synod Fathers in the Sistine chapel. Paul VI did not attend this celebration because of an "indisposition," however.

Besides the changes that were already in force since the 1964 and 1967 Instructions (Mass celebrated facing the people in Italian including the Canon, fewer genuflections and signs of the cross, etc.), the "normative" Mass that Fr Bugnini celebrated with a large choir added other new elements: a longer Liturgy of the Word (three

---

5. *The Memoirs of Louis Bouyer: From Youth and Conversion to Vatican II, the Liturgical Reform, and After* (Kettering, OH: Angelico Press, 2015), 221–22.
6. Ibid., 223.

readings total), a transformed Offertory, a new Eucharistic Prayer (the third), and a great number of hymns.

During the four general congregations devoted to the liturgy (October 21–25), cardinals and bishops made many comments on this "normative" Mass and on the liturgical reform in general. All told, sixty-three cardinals, bishops, and religious superiors general commented on the subject and a further nineteen submitted written comments. There was a diversity of opinion.[7] "Of sixty-three orators," Fr Caprile reported, "thirty-six explicitly expressed, in the warmest, most enthusiastic, and unreserved terms," their agreement with the reform underway and its results. Some bishops even wanted further changes, such as the possibility of receiving communion in the hand, that of using ordinary bread for communion, and the preparation of a specific Mass for youth, etc.

Yet the general tone was more prudent, if not reserved or even critical. The English-speaking bishops met at the English College to define a common position on the "normative" Mass. On October 25, at the Synod, Cardinal Heenan, Archbishop of Westminster, took the floor to accuse the *Consilium* of technicism and intellectualism and to blame it for lacking pastoral sense. More significant yet, in the sense that they came from the highest authority in the Church after the pope, were the words of Cardinal Cicognani, Secretary of State, who on the very same day asked for an end to liturgical changes "lest the faithful be confused."

Twice during the debates on the liturgy, the participants were invited to express their opinion through a vote.[8] On October 25, they answered four questions that Paul VI had specifically posed: on

7. Regarding the synod debates, see the articles published each day in *L'Osservatore Romano*, the long report published in *Notitiae* (1967): 353–70, and two journalistic chronicles: Giovanni Caprile, "Il Sinodo dei vescovi," *Civiltà Cattolica* 2820 (16 December 1967): 595–603 and Henri Fesquet, whose articles published in *Le Monde* are collected in ibid., *Le Journal du premier synode catholique* (Paris: Robert Morel, 1967). See also Bugnini, *Reform*, 346–59. For a scholarly analysis, see Christiaan Kappes, "The 'Missa Normativa' of 1967: Its History and Principles as Applied to the Liturgy of the Mass," doctoral thesis (SLD), Pontificium Athenaeum S. Anselmi de Urbe, 2012.

8. *Notitiae* 3 (1967): 353–70.

the three new Eucharistic Prayers, on two changes in the formula of consecration, and on the possibility of replacing the Niceno-Constantinopolitan creed with the Apostles' Creed. Eight more questions were posed on October 27, particularly on the normative Mass and on the Divine Office draft.

Leaving aside a detailed analysis of these twelve votes, it is noteworthy that for half of them (two out of the pope's four questions and four out of eight of the remainder), the required two-thirds majority was not reached. There were 187 voters; the two-thirds majority was therefore 124. For some of the votes, the tally was far from it, with the *non placet* (nays) and *placet juxta modum* (approval on condition of modifications) having a broad margin. For example, regarding the suppression of the phrase *Mysterium fidei* in the consecration formula, there were only 93 *placet*. More spectacular yet was the refusal to give unreserved approval to the general structure of the normative Mass: 71 *placet*; 43 *non placet*; 62 *placet juxta modum*; 4 abstentions.[9]

A few months later Fr Bugnini acknowledged to *Consilium* consultors and members that "the response of the bishops was not unanimous. The votes in the Synod went to some extent contrary to what the Consilium wanted [*contro il 'Consilium'*]."[10]

Lercaro's "Destitution"

This public disavowal of the *Consilium's* work was one of the causes that led to Cardinal Lercaro's destitution.

In August 1966, Cardinal Lercaro, who was reaching the age limit of 75 imposed on bishops and curial officials, had presented his resignation to the pope. Paul VI had asked him to continue in his functions as both archbishop of Bologna and president of the *Consilium*. Nevertheless, Paul VI named one of his close collaborators, Msgr Poma, as coadjutor in the archdiocese of Bologna in June 1967.

9. The conclusion drawn by Archbishop Marini, who quotes none of the votes' results, is puzzling: "The Synod of Bishops approved the work of the reform being carried out by the Consilium by a wide majority, in spite of a few difficulties," Marini, 138.

10. Allocution of Fr Bugnini, April 23, 1968, in id., *Reform*, 175.

Then, unexpectedly for the cardinal, Paul VI wrote to Lercaro on January 9, 1968 to tell him that he accepted his resignation from the *Consilium*. The pope sent him a representative on the following 27th, whose mission was to secure the cardinal archbishop's resignation [from the See of Bologna], which the latter, with a heavy heart, submitted on February 12.

One of Lercaro's close collaborators, Don Lorenzo Bedeschi, presented this double resignation as a "destitution."[11] History, in the main, has accepted this view.[12] Diverse reasons led to this double destitution: Cardinal Lercaro's controversial pastoral policies in Bologna, his links to the Communist municipality (he agreed to being made an "honorary citizen"), his appeal against American bombing in Vietnam. Yet his management of the liturgical reform was also questioned. In 1967 the backlash linked to Casini's pamphlet and the criticism leveled at the "normative" Mass had brought to light the opposition to the work of the *Consilium*, whose president he had been since 1964.

One may therefore say that Paul VI attempted to regain control of the liturgical reform in early 1968. Just as he officially accepted the resignation of the *Consilium* president, he simultaneously asked Cardinal Larraona to resign from the Congregation of Rites. On the same day Cardinal Gut, a Benedictine monk who was already a *Consilium* member, became its president as well the new prefect of the Congregation of Rites. This double nomination anticipated the fusion of the two organisms, which would occur the following year.

Paul VI still had full confidence in Bugnini, however. During the audience that followed Lercaro's resignation, Paul VI told Bugnini: "Now you alone are left. I urge you to be very patient and very prudent. I assure you once again of my complete confidence." Fr Bug-

---

11. Lorenzo Bedeschi, *Il Cardinale destituito. Documenti sul "caso" Lercaro* (Turin: Gribaudi, 1968).

12. Luigi Accatoli, "La figura di Paolo VI nell'opinione pubblica italiana," in *Paul VI et la modernité dans l'Église* (Rome: École française de Rome, 1984), 209–23; Nazario Sauro Onofri, *Le due anime del cardinale Lercaro* (Bologna: Cappelli Editore, 1987); Giuseppe Alberigo, "Un vescovo e un popolo," in *Araldo del Vangelo. Studi sull'episcopato e sull'archivio di Giacomo Lercaro a Bologna. 1952–1968*, ed. N. Buonasorte (Bologna: Il Mulino, 2004), 103–32.

nini answered: "Holy Father, the reform will continue as long as Your Holiness retains this confidence. As soon as it lessens, the reform will come to a halt."[13]

Towards the "New Mass"

The *Consilium* put the "new Mass" project, which had been roundly criticized at the October 1967 Synod, back on the drawing board.

We have seen that Paul VI had been unable to attend the first experiment of the "normative" Mass. A report prepared under Fr Bugnini's direction had been presented to him on December 11, 1967. During an audience on January 4, 1968, he asked Fr Bugnini to organize three new "experimental" celebrations, to take place in his presence in the Matilda chapel on the second floor of the Apostolic Palace.[14]

These three "normative" Masses were all celebrated in the late afternoon by one of Bugnini's two closest collaborators, each with a different Eucharistic prayer, but in different modes of celebration: on January 11, a read Mass with hymns celebrated by Fr Carlo Braga; on January 12, an "entirely read Mass with participation of the faithful" celebrated by Fr Gottardo Pasqualetti; and on January 13, a sung Mass, once again celebrated by Fr Braga.

Each of the celebrations was attended by about thirty people besides the pope: the cardinal Secretary of State, different members of the Curia, several members of the *Consilium*, two religious women, and four laymen (two men and two women).

These three experimental celebrations in the presence of the pope presented a few differences with the "normative" Mass that had been celebrated before the Synod a few months earlier, in particular by the introduction of a "Sign of Peace" that all in attendance exchanged after the instruction "Give each other the Peace."

After each of the Masses, the pope welcomed some of the participants along with Fr Bugnini in his private library to share impressions and comments on what had been done in the celebration. On

13. Bugnini, *Reform*, xxviii.
14. Ibid., 359–64.

the following January 22, Paul VI provided his own written comments during an audience he granted to Fr Bugnini.[15] The pope made seven suggestions, asking in particular that the Offertory should be given more prominence since it "should be the part of the Mass in which ... [the faithful's] activity is more direct and obvious." He also asked that the expression *Mysterium fidei* should be maintained at the end of the formula of consecration, "as a concluding acclamation of the celebrant, to be repeated by the faithful" and that the triple *Agnus Dei* invocation should be retained. Paul VI once again echoed some "authoritative persons" who asked that the last Gospel at the end of Mass (the prologue of the Gospel according to St. John) should be restored. Lastly, he asked that "the words of consecration ... not be recited simply as a narrative but with the special, conscious emphasis given them by a celebrant who knows he is speaking and acting 'in the person of Christ.'"

Also on January 22, Paul VI asked that the *schema* of the new Mass be sent, after revision, to all the Curia dicastery heads, a number of whom had expressed reservations or criticisms of the Synod "normative" Mass. "We must win them over and make allies of them," the pope explicitly said, even if this entailed the argument from authority: "You saw, didn't you, what happened when St. Joseph's name was introduced into the Canon? First, everyone was against it. Then one fine morning Pope John decided to insert it and made this known; then everyone applauded, even those who had said they were opposed to it."[16]

The following May 23, Cardinal Gut, prefect of the Congregation of Rites and president of the *Consilium*, published a decree authorizing the use of the three new Eucharistic Prayers and of eight new Prefaces.[17] They could be used starting on August 15, 1968. Once again, the traditional rite of the Mass was emended on important points before the new rite was completed and promulgated.

15. For the complete text of the pope's note, see ibid., 364–65.
16. Ibid., 369, n. 30. To the objection "And if the response is still negative?," the pope answered: "Don't worry, I have the final say," ibid.
17. Decree *Prece eucharistica* of 23 May 1968, DOL 241.

On June 2, 1968, the revised draft of the new *Ordo Missae* was sent, as Paul VI had intended, to fourteen curial cardinals (Congregation prefects and Secretariat presidents). Fr Bugnini was to report that "of the fourteen cardinals involved, two did not reply, seven sent observations, and five said simply that they had no remarks to make or were 'very pleased' with the *schema*."[18]

It is noteworthy that the *Institutio Generalis Missalis Romani* (the "General Instruction of the Roman Missal"), which was to preface the new *Ordo Missae*, was not sent to these cardinals, not even to the Congregation for the Doctrine of the Faith. This *Institutio*, which was made up of eight chapters and put together by a study group directed by Fr Carlo Braga, presented itself as "at once [a] doctrinal, pastoral, and rubrical" treatment of the new Mass.[19] Certain articles of this *Institutio* would come under criticism, as we shall see.

Paul VI had the revised draft and the cardinals' responses examined by two of his close collaborators, Msgr Carlo Colombo, his private theologian, and Bishop Manziana of Crema. Then he read and reread the draft himself, inserting marginal notes and underscoring the text in red and blue pencil, though without seeking to impose his views. On September 22, 1968, he gave the annotated draft back to Fr Bugnini with the following written remark: "I ask you to take account of these observations, exercising a free and carefully weighed judgment."[20]

From October 8 to 17, the *Consilium*'s eleventh plenary session met to work on the Mass, but also on other rites (notably the Blessing of an Abbot and Religious Profession). Paul VI hosted the participants on October 14 and gave a long allocution. Its tone was graver than on any previous occasion.[21] The pope issued several warnings: "Reform of the liturgy must not be taken to be a repudiation of the sacred patrimony of past ages and a reckless welcoming

18. Bugnini, *Reform*, 372.
19. Ibid., 386.
20. Ibid., 377. Bugnini further specifies whether, and how, the pope's observations and proposals were adopted.
21. Latin text: *L'Osservatore Romano*, 16 October 1968, *AAS* 60 (1968): 732–37, and *Notitiae* 4 (1968): 335–40. For an English translation see *DOL* 92.

of every conceivable novelty." He insisted on the "ecclesial and hier-archic character of the liturgy":

> The rites and prayer formularies must not be regarded as a private matter, left up to individuals, a parish, a diocese, or a nation, but as the property of the whole Church, because they express the living voice of its prayer. No one, then, is permitted to change these formularies, to introduce new ones, or to substitute others in their place.

More than this, Paul VI for the first time publicly deplored abuses committed by certain conferences of bishops:

> This results at times even in conferences of bishops going too far on their own initiative in liturgical matters. Another result is arbitrary experimentation in the introduction of rites that are flagrantly in conflict with the norms established by the Church. Anyone can see that this way of acting not only scandalizes the conscience of the faithful but does harm to the orderly accomplishment of liturgical reform, which demands of all concerned prudence, vigilance, and above all discipline.

The *Novus Ordo Missae* (N.O.M.)

On November 6, 1968, Paul VI, after rereading the new *Ordo Missae* one more time, gave it his written "approbation." The Apostolic Constitution *Missale Romanum* of April 3, 1969 was announced in Consistory on the following April 28 and presented to the press on May 2, the publication day of the new *Ordo Missae*,[22] which was soon called the "new Mass" or the N.O.M. (*Novus Ordo Missae*).

A new missal, soon commonly termed the "Paul VI Missal," was about to succeed the Roman Missal codified by Saint Pius V.

The rite of the Mass was now "simplified." In fact, we have seen that between the traditional Missal used on the eve of the Council in 1962 and the 1969 Missal, there had been a succession of transformations: the N.O.M. was not a pure innovation. In some of its formulations, the *Institutio Generalis* was far more innovative. It is

---

22. *Ordo Missae* (Vatican City: Typis Polyglottis Vaticanis, 1969), 174 pages.

worth noting that this lengthy "General Presentation" was not submitted to the Congregation for the Doctrine of the Faith before publication. A number of infelicitous expressions provoked fierce criticism.

The "new Mass" was actually not as new as was claimed. Indeed, considering prior Instructions, it synthesized and made official the changes that had already been taking place: a more communal penitential part of the Mass; more numerous and diverse Sunday readings spread out over a three-year cycle; a restored "universal prayer"; new Prefaces; a changed Offertory; three new Eucharistic Prayers added to the ancient Roman Canon to be used at the celebrant's choice; modified words of consecration, identical in all four Eucharistic Prayers; the *Pater noster* said by the whole congregation, no longer by the priest alone; suppression of many genuflections, signs of the cross, and bows.

The Path to Communion in the Hand

As we have seen, in 1965 Cardinal Lercaro, president of the *Consilium*, considered "placing the host in the open hands of the faithful" to be a deplorable and fanciful initiative. Neither the 1969 Missal nor the *Institutio Generalis* provided for the possibility of receiving communion in the hand. Yet the practice had already spread in several countries. The Congregation for Divine Worship therefore published a lengthy Instruction on the topic dated May 29, 1969.[23]

As Jean Madiran was later to point out,[24] this Instruction looks like a composite document. On the one hand, the Instruction uses different arguments (theological, spiritual, and practical) to defend the traditional manner of receiving communion and states that it must remain the norm: "In view of the overall contemporary situation of the Church, this manner of distributing communion must be retained. Not only is it based on a practice handed down over

---

23. Instruction *Memoriale Domini, DOL* 260.

24. Jean Madiran, "Le processus de la communion dans la main," *Itinéraires* 163 (May 1972): 213–21.

many centuries, but above all it signifies the faithful's reverence for the Eucharist."

In support of maintaining this tradition, the same document published the results of a survey conducted among all Latin-rite bishops. Without getting into the detail of the answers given to the three questions, we give here only those given to the first question: "Do you think that a positive response should be given to the request to allow the rite of receiving communion in the hand?"

In favor: 567
Opposed: 1,253
In favor with reservations: 315
Invalid votes: 20

On the basis of the survey's results, the Instruction prescribed the following: "[Pope Paul VI's] judgment is not to change the long-accepted manner of administering communion to the faithful. The Apostolic See earnestly urges bishops, priests, and faithful, therefore, to obey conscientiously the prevailing law, now recon-firmed. . . ."

Yet in the second part, which is shorter and looks like an add-on, the same text granted to episcopal conferences the possibility of authorizing communion in the hand:

Wherever the contrary practice, that is, of communion in the hand, has already come into use, the Apostolic See . . . entrusts to the same conferences of bishops the duty and task of evaluating any possible special circumstances. This, however, is with the pro-viso both that they prevent any possible lack of reverence or false ideas about the Eucharist from being engendered in the attitudes of the people and that they carefully eliminate anything else unac-ceptable.

Cardinal Oddi reports that, from a concern not to restrict the freedom of episcopal conferences and to respect the diversity of opinions, Paul VI refused to impose a single law in the matter, although he was personally opposed to communion in the hand.[25]

25. Cardinal Oddi to the author, 18 August 1992.

In the event, what had been a limited concession in 1969 has become the norm in a great many countries and parishes.[†]

Pierre Lemaire, director of the review *Défense du Foyer* and of the Éditions Saint-Michel and an activist in defense of the family and of the catechism, voiced a complaint on the subject in Rome. In 1969, during one of his many visits to the Vatican, he was received by Cardinal Seper, prefect of the Congregation for the Doctrine of the Faith, and by Cardinal Wright, new prefect of the Congregation for Clergy. He gave each of them a *Pro memoria* exposing "the dramatic and catastrophic confusion in which France finds herself" and the "fundamental points" that were introducing a "rupture" between Catholics faithful to the Holy See and the clergy. Pierre Lemaire underscored the "crisis" that the liturgical question had precipitated:

> The aberrant liturgies invading our churches—now as bare as Protestant houses of worship—are having a disastrous effect. Communion in the hand, often distributed in baskets to all takers, represents the nadir of the innumerable profanations spreading in progressive parishes because of the multiplying sacrilegious communions of the "faithful" who never go to confession. In this climate, the new "Ordo Missae" is received not as a step forward but as the herald of further degradations, since the clergy, which is badly formed and badly taught in wayward seminaries, is open to any and all experiments.[26]

The Congregation for Divine Worship

The promulgation of the new Missal did not mean that the implementation of the liturgical reform was at an end; it indicated that the reform was at its height.

Paul VI, in a consistory held on April 28, 1969, announced that the venerable Congregation of Rites was to be divided into two Congregations: the Congregation for Divine Worship focusing on

---

[†] For a thorough presentation, see Most Rev. Juan Rodolfo Laise, *Communion in the Hand: Documents and History* (Boonville, NY: Preserving Christian Publications, 2011).—*Ed.*

26. *Pro memoria* dated 18 September 1969, Lemaire family archives.

the liturgy in particular and the Congregation for the Causes of Saints that was to handle beatification and canonization causes.

The Apostolic Constitution *Sacra Rituum Congregatio* of May 8, 1969 established two new Congregations. The *Consilium* no longer existed as an autonomous body: it was integrated into the new Congregation for Divine Worship under the title "Special Commission for the Implementation of the Liturgical Reform."

Cardinal Gut was named prefect and Fr Bugnini secretary of this new Congregation. Although his title remained unchanged ("secretary") and he was not yet given the prelature granting him the title "Monsignor,"[27] Fr Bugnini was completely integrated into the Curia. He left the old Palazzo Santa Marta buildings to set up with his collaborators on the fourth floor of the nice modern Palazzo dei Congregazioni, at 10 Piazza Pio XII.

He now belonged to a Curia dicastery, which strengthened his authority but at the same time reduced his autonomy. The new Congregation "was to be organized according to the structures and regulations of the other curial departments."[28] Only seven of the forty *Consilium* bishops stayed on as members of the new Congregation and the number of consultors was considerably reduced: only nineteen remained.

Cardinal Gut, prefect of this new Congregation, tried to channel the liturgical ferment that had been disrupting the lives of the faithful in many parishes. In an interview sometime after the creation of the Congregation for Divine Worship, he announced that "stricter measures" would be taken. He said: "At present the limits of the conciliar Constitution on the Liturgy have been vastly overrun in many areas. Many elements have been introduced, with or without authorization, which go beyond the liturgy *schema*."[29] He hoped that this "fever of experimentation [would] soon come to an end" and, surprisingly, he (respectfully) lay part of the blame at the feet of the pope: "These unauthorized initiatives often could no longer be

27. Canon Martimort had been named prelate of the pontifical household already in 1967.
28. Marini, 141.
29. Interview granted to the *Linzer Kirchenblatt*, 20 July 1969.

stopped because they had spread too far abroad. In his great goodness and wisdom the Holy Father then gave in, often against his own will."

The Ottaviani Intervention

The new *Ordo Missae* was to come into effect on November 30, 1969, the first Sunday of Advent.

Even before this date, however, the severest doctrinal critiques proliferated, some with the support of eminent authorities. They aimed both at the *Ordo Missae* and at the *Institutio Generalis* prefacing it.[30] Even a review so attached to *romanità* as *La Pensée catholique* published, under collective authorships ("a group of theologians" and "a group of canonists"), two lengthy critiques of the new *Ordo Missae*.[31] The group of theologians lamented that the new Mass "completely disregards the doctrine of the Council of Trent on the Mass: *incruens sacrificium*" and deemed that it "is not in conformity with the tradition of the Roman Church."

The most glaring opposition came from a *Short Critical Study of the New Order of Mass*.[32] This *Short Critical Study*, which is dated to the feast of Corpus Christi (June 5, 1969) but was only published a few months later, was unsigned at the time. The letter that Cardinals Ottaviani and Bacci wrote to Paul VI to introduce the *Study* indicates that it was composed by "a select group of bishops, theologians, liturgists and pastors of souls." It later transpired that a lay-

---

30. The best edition of this controverted text and of its successively emended versions is that by Maurizio Barba, *Institutio generalis Missalis Romani. Textus, synopsis, variationes* (Vatican: Libreria Editrice Vaticana, 2006).

31. *La Pensée catholique* 122 (1969): 5–47.

32. The first widely available English translation of the *Short Critical Study* was that prepared in the early 1970s for the Lumen Gentium Foundation (no publication date given). The version used here, which has superseded the 1970s translation, is *The Ottaviani Intervention: Short Critical Study of the New Order of Mass by Alfredo Cardinal Ottaviani, Antonio Cardinal Bacci, A Group of Roman Theologians*, trans. Anthony Cekada (Rockford, IL: TAN, 1992; new ed., West Chester, OH: Philothea Press, 2010). It has since come to be widely known in English as *The Ottaviani Intervention*. The English translation used for the *Institutio Generalis* is that of *DOL* 208, translating the fourth edition of 27 March 1975, with notes indicating the wording of the first edition of 1969.

woman, the Italian writer Cristina Campo (1923–1977), and the Dominican theologian Michel Guérard des Lauriers, professor at the Dominican-run Pontifical University Angelicum, had an essential role in writing this document.

The *Short Critical Study* began by questioning the definition of the Mass that the *Institutio Generalis* presented at chapter 3, §7: "The Lord's supper or Mass is the sacred assembly or congregation of the people of God gathering together, with a priest presiding, in order to celebrate the memorial of the Lord." The term "supper" was taken up again at §§ 8, 48, 55, and 56. The *Short Critical Study* deplored this in the following terms:

None of this in the very least implies:
- The Real Presence.
- The reality of the Sacrifice.
- The sacramental function of the priest who consecrates.
- The intrinsic value of the Eucharistic Sacrifice independent of the presence of the "assembly."

The *Short Critical Study* spoke in scholastic categories when it also regretted that the "ends or purposes" of the Mass (ultimate, ordinary, immanent) did not appear clearly. It also questioned the formulas of consecration and the place of the priest in the new rite: a "minimized, changed, and falsified" role.

This relentless critique ended in a total rejection of the "new Mass" which "due to the countless liberties it implicitly authorizes, cannot but be a sign of division—a liturgy which teems with insinuations or manifest errors against the integrity of the Catholic Faith."

Two cardinals, Bacci and Ottaviani, who no longer had any official functions in the Curia, agreed to present this *Short Critical Study* to the pope. They did so in a letter accompanying the document. In this letter, dated September 25, 1969, the two cardinals judged that "the *Novus Ordo Missae*—considering the new elements susceptible to widely different interpretations which are implied or taken for granted—represents, both as a whole and in its details, a striking departure from the Catholic theology of the Mass." In consequence, they were asking for the new rite of the Mass to be "abrogated."

Although other cardinals and bishops had been approached to sign this plea, none made up their mind to take that step. Cardinal Siri, Archbishop of Genoa, thought that this *Study* was "more Bacci's doing than Ottaviani's" and that Cardinal Ottaviani gave his signature when the text had already been printed.[33] Cardinal Siri added that he himself "would not have added his signature if he'd been asked."

Generally speaking, Cardinal Siri's views on the liturgical reform were simple:

> The Council did not ask for any such revolution. The liturgical reform was done, the pope approved it, and that's enough: I take the position of obedience, which is always owed to the pope. If he had asked me, I think I might have made some observations—several. But once a law has been approved, there is only one thing left to do: obey.[34]

The *Short Critical Study* came to Paul VI's knowledge in September 1969;[†] the press began to trumpet the story in the following month.[35] The pope sent the *Study* to the Congregation for the Doctrine of the Faith for review. Cardinal Seper, the Congregation prefect, gave his answer by November 12: "The pamphlet *Breve esame* ... contains many superficial, exaggerated, inaccurate, biased, and false statements."[36]

Jean Madiran had been the first in France to publish the letter of Cardinals Bacci and Ottaviani.[37] He was also the first to publish

---

33. E. Cavaterra, *Il Prefetto del Sant'Offizio. Le opere e i giorni del cardinal Ottaviani* (Milan: Mursia, 1990), 118.

34. Cardinal Siri, ibid., 117.

† The document, which had appeared in the Italian press on September 14, was placed into the pope's hands with a covering letter signed by Ottaviani and Bacci on September 29. See Alcuin Reid, "After *Sacrosanctum Concilium*—Continuity or Rupture?," in *T&T Clark Companion to Liturgy* (London/New York: Bloomsbury T&T Clark, 2016), 297–98.—*Ed.*

35. On October 30, 1969, *Il Messaggero* bore the title "Cardinals Ottaviani and Bacci: the new Mass is 'heretical' and 'sacrilegious.'"

36. Quoted in Bugnini, *Reform*, 287.

37. *Itinéraires* 138 (December 1969): 22–24.

the French version of the *Short Critical Study of the New Order of Mass*.[38]

On the other hand, in 1970 Pierre Lemaire published as a supplement to *Défense du Foyer* 111 a small brochure under the sober title *Note doctrinale sur le Nouvel Ordo Missae* ("Doctrinal Note on the New *Ordo Missae*"). This forty-four-page brochure was commissioned, as the text says, "by the Knights of Our Lady," an organization to which Pierre Lemaire belonged. In fact, the main writer of this "Note" was Dom Gérard Lafond, the Order's chaplain and a monk at the abbey of Saint Wandrille where he taught Sacred Scripture.

The *Doctrinal Note*, while it did express some criticisms regarding the translation of the new *Ordo Missae* then circulating in France, came to the defense of the new Mass's orthodoxy. The *Doctrinal Note* also expressed the opinion that "Cardinal Ottaviani cannot have given his approval to the *Short Critical Study*; they probably refrained from reading it to him."[39]

Dom Lafond's study had been sent to different authorities for review before being published by Pierre Lemaire along with excerpts of the responses they had sent in. Cardinal Journet had praised these "solid, luminous, balanced pages." Fr Louis Bouyer, a renowned theologian and liturgical specialist, found the work "quite good." Msgr Agustoni, Cardinal Ottaviani's secretary, praised what he called "a serious, deep, serene work accomplished in the eye of the storm."

Then, the following month, Pierre Lemaire published a letter from Cardinal Ottaviani that caused a sensation.[40] This letter, which was addressed to Dom Lafond to thank him for the *Note doctrinale*, was in near complete counterpoint to the *Short Critical Study* published a few months before. In this letter Cardinal Ottaviani characterized Dom Lafond's *Note doctrinale* as "remarkable for

---

38. *Itinéraires* 141 (March 1970): 219–51.

39. Cardinal Ottaviani had been blind for some years.

40. Ottaviani to Lafond, 17 February 1970, Lemaire family archives. Published in *Défense du Foyer* (March 1970), then picked up in the mainstream press (*Le Monde*, *La Croix*, *Le Figaro*).

its objectivity and its dignity of expression." He also deplored the publicity that had been given to his letter to Paul VI: "I regret that my name has been abused in a direction I did not want through the publication of a letter addressed to the Holy Father, without my having authorized anyone to publish it."

Above all, Cardinal Ottaviani expressed his satisfaction with the allocutions Paul VI had given in general audience on November 19 and 26, 1969, and judged that henceforth "no one can be scandalized anymore," even though "there is need for prudent and intelligent catechesis to remove a few legitimate perplexities that the text may arouse."

Paul VI's Corrections and Rectifications

To Jean Madiran, the letter from Cardinal Ottaviani to Dom Lafond seemed to be a provocation against the truth. A lively polemic ensued. Jean Madiran published a brochure in response to the *Note doctrinale*, its author, and Pierre Lemaire who had published it. He also questioned the authenticity of the letter from Cardinal Ottaviani to Pierre Lafond.[41] This he did in highly polemical terms, judging that, in this whole business, Dom Lafond and Pierre Lemaire had been "duped and manipulated."

In reality and according to diverse well-known attestations, one may consider that Cardinal Ottaviani had most certainly first approved the *Short Critical Study*, of which he was not the author. Then, a few months later, he gave his approval to Dom Lafond's *Note doctrinale*. His position regarding the "new Mass" (which he went on to celebrate) had changed because in the meantime Paul VI had provided corrections and rectifications of no small import.

Indeed, at the time neither the enthusiastic partisans of the new Mass and of the liturgical reform nor its most determined adversaries paid sufficient attention to what the pope did and said to rectify and correct the texts he had first approved and promulgated.

On the one hand, there were the allocutions given during the

---

41. Jean Madiran, "Sur la lettre du cardinal Ottaviani à Paul VI," *Itinéraires* 142, suppl. April 1970.

general audiences on November 19 and 26, 1969, two Wednesdays in a row. They were entirely devoted to the new Mass. Paul VI had explained the reasons for the changes in the rite and reaffirmed that it substantially "is and will remain the Mass it always has been": a sacrifice offered by the priest "in a different mode, that is, unbloodily and sacramentally, as his perpetual memorial until his final coming."[42]

He acknowledged that abandoning Latin was a "great sacrifice," necessary for a better "understanding of prayer." He also asserted: "Finally, close examination will reveal that the fundamental plan of the Mass in its theological and spiritual import remains what it always has been." The phrase "close examination" is worth noting: it acknowledged that continuity between the "old" Mass and the "new" was not obvious or immediately apparent.

There were also the important corrections to the *Institutio Generalis*. Under the pressure of the moment, so to speak, Cardinal Gut and Fr Bugnini published a "Declaration" to specify that the *Institutio* "is not to be considered as a doctrinal or dogmatic document but as a pastoral and ritual instruction describing the celebration and each of its parts."[43]

Then there were the additions and corrections made to many articles of the *Instructio* itself.[44] These are easy to pick out in a synoptic comparison of the 1969 *editio typica* and the 1970 *editio typica*.[45] In the first place a lengthy, fifteen-paragraph *Proemium* ("Preamble") had been added; it repeated the traditional Catholic doctrine of the Mass as a propitiatory sacrifice and notably cited the definitions of the Council of Trent several times. The chapters of the *Instructio* themselves had been corrected in several points by addition or by a different formulation. The famous §7 which, in the 1969 edition, gave a more than incomplete definition of the Mass, was

42. Paul VI, Address to a General Audience, November 19, 1969, *DOL* 211.1759. The next quotations are from the November 26 Address, *DOL* 212.1762–63.

43. *Notitiae* 5 (1969): 417.

44. "Variationes in 'Institutionem generalem Missalis romani' inductae," *Notitiae* 54 (May 1970): 177–90.

45. See the synoptic tables in Barba, *Institutio* (see p. 141, n. 30 above), 389–667.

corrected to yield a more complete and more theologically accurate definition. While it defined it again as a gathering and memorial— "At Mass or the Lord's Supper, the people of God are called together, with a priest presiding and acting in the person of Christ, to celebrate the memorial of the Lord"—the new text defined it as a sacrifice also, and insisted on transubstantiation and the Real Presence: "For at the celebration of the Mass, which perpetuates the sacrifice of the Cross, Christ is really present to the assembly gathered in his name; he is present in the person of the minister, in his own word, and indeed substantially and permanently under the Eucharistic elements."

The typical edition of the *Missale Romanum* published in Rome in 1970 also included substantial corrections, even though its structure remained unchanged. In fact, within a few months, the text of the new *Ordo Missae* as well as that of the *Institutio Generalis* had undergone revisions that were not merely marginal changes. These did not satisfy those who had for several months been multiplying criticisms on both form and substance. On the other hand, some were convinced and changed their views; for instance, Fr Luc Lefèvre retracted his initial critical stance and, in an editorial in *La Pensée catholique*, affirmed: "All the ambiguities have definitively and officially been set aside, then. *Bene. Recte. Optime.*"[46]

An "Obligatory" New Mass—with Exceptions

There is no need here to recount how the new Mass was made obligatory in the Church universal, except to mention that in some countries decisions at the national level were made before prescriptions were issued from Rome. The Holy See granted a few derogations too, a process in which Fr Bugnini was closely involved.

The Apostolic Constitution *Missale Romanum* was to go into effect on November 30, 1969, the First Sunday in Advent. The bishops of France, gathered in a Plenary Assembly in Lourdes, decided in a decree adopted on November 12 that the new *Ordo Missae* would

---

46. *La Pensée catholique* 128 (1970): 6.

be "obligatory as of January 1, 1970" (article 1).[47] The decree foresaw only two exceptions, termed "particular cases":

> Art. 10. Elderly priests who celebrate Mass "without the people" and for whom it would be too difficult to become accustomed to the new *Ordo Missae* and to the new texts of the Roman Missal and of the *Ordo lectionum missae* may, with the consent of their Ordinary, follow the current rites and texts.
> Art. 11. Other particular cases, e.g., concerning ailing or infirm priests, will be submitted to the Ordinary.

But the long and necessary work of translation caused the celebration of the Mass in French in all churches to be postponed until the First Sunday of Advent 1970 (November 29).

Between Paul VI's promulgation of the Constitution on April 3, 1969 and the official implementation of the "new Mass" in French on November 29, 1970, over a year and a half had passed. During this period, a number of anarchical liturgies and "liturgical experiments" had kept developing in a great many French parishes.

The Congregation for Divine Worship issued a decree dated March 26, 1970, signed by Cardinal Gut and Fr Bugnini. This decree "promulgates and declares to be the *editio typica*" the "new edition of the Roman Missal." The same decree specified that "the Latin edition may be put into use as soon as it is published" and that "as to the vernacular editions, the conferences of bishops are given the responsibility for their preparation and for setting the effective date for their use, after due confirmation by the Apostolic See."[48]

At this date, therefore, as far as the Holy See was concerned, it was merely a matter of permitting the use of the new Missal in the Latin edition (which was still under press) and in the vernacular translations once they had been produced and had received the approval of the Holy See.

A little over a year later, on June 14, 1971, the same Congregation issued a more imperative notification:

---

47. *Documentation catholique* 1552 (7 December 1969), 1078–79.
48. Decree *Celebrationes eucharisticae*, 16 March 1970, AAS 62 (1970): 554; *Notitiae* 6 (1970): 169. English translation, *DOL* 213.

[The episcopal] conferences should, however, settle on a definite date when translations . . . *may or must* be put into use in whole or in part. From the date on which the translated texts *become obligatory* for celebrations in the vernacular, *only* the revised form of the Mass and the Liturgy of the Hours *will be allowed*, even for those who continue to use Latin.[49]

In a little over a year, the Congregation for Divine Worship had moved from possibility to obligation. This obligatory character was accentuated by the only derogation granted: "those who because of their advanced years or illness find serious difficulties in using the new Order of Mass in the Roman Missal" would be able to continue using the older *Ordo*. But this concession was granted on two conditions: the celebrants who maintained the ancient rite were to do so "with the consent of the Ordinary" and "only in celebrations without a congregation."

Many took this notification, which was published in *L'Osservatore Romano* on June 16, 1971, as a prohibition to celebrate according to the ancient rite of the Mass from then on. Three weeks later, July 6, 1971, the *Times* of London published a petition from many British and overseas personalities who, in the name of culture and civilization, wished "to call to the attention of the Holy See, the appalling responsibility it would incur in the history of the human spirit were it to refuse to allow the Traditional Mass to survive, even though this survival took place side by side with other liturgical forms."

The petition had an international impact.[50] Not all the signatories were Catholic; some were not even Christian. Among them were notably Agatha Christie, Graham Greene, Yehudi Menuhin, Jorge Luis Borges, Roger Caillois, Julien Green, Henry de Montherlant, Augusto del Noce. The list was prestigious and, it is said, impressed Paul VI.

49. Notification *Instructione de Constitutione*, 14 June 1971; *AAS* 63 (1971): 712–15; *Notitiae* 7 (1971): 215–17; *DOL* 216.1771.

50. *The London Times*, 6 July 1971. [The full text of the appeal reads: "If some senseless decree were to order the total or partial destruction of basilicas or cathedrals, then obviously it would be the educated—whatever their personal beliefs—who would rise up in horror to oppose such a possibility. Now the fact is that basilicas and cathedrals were built so as to celebrate a rite which, until a few months ago,

Shortly thereafter, in an audience granted by Paul VI on October 29, 1971, Cardinal Heenan, archbishop of Westminster and president of the Catholic Bishops' Conference of England and Wales, asked in the name of the British episcopate for the possibility of the older liturgy to be used by certain groups.

The indult was granted by November 5:

> This faculty may be granted provided that groups make the request for reasons of genuine devotion, and provided that the permission does not disturb or damage the general communion of the faithful. For this reason, the permission is limited to certain groups on special occasions; at all regular parish and other community Masses, the Order of the Mass given in the new Roman Missal should be used. Since the Eucharist is the sacrament of unity, it is necessary that the use of the Order of Mass given in the former Missal should not become a sign or cause of disunity in the Catholic community. For this reason, agreement among the bish-

---

constituted a living tradition. We are referring to the Roman Catholic Mass. Yet, according to the latest information in Rome, there is a plan to obliterate that Mass by the end of the current year. One of the axioms of contemporary publicity, religious as well as secular, is that modern man in general, and intellectuals in particular, have become intolerant of all forms of tradition and are anxious to suppress them and put something else in their place. But, like many other affirmations of our publicity machines, this axiom is false. Today, as in times gone by, educated people are in the vanguard where recognition of the value of tradition is concerned, and are the first to raise the alarm when it is threatened. We are not at this moment considering the religious or spiritual experience of millions of individuals. The rite in question, in its magnificent Latin text, has also inspired a host of priceless achievements in the arts—not only mystical works, but works by poets, philosophers, musicians, architects, painters and sculptors in all countries and epochs. Thus, it belongs to universal culture as well as to churchmen and formal Christians. In the materialistic and technocratic civilisation that is increasingly threatening the life of mind and spirit in its original creative expression—the word—it seems particularly inhuman to deprive man of word-forms in one of their most grandiose manifestations. The signatories of this appeal, which is entirely ecumenical and nonpolitical, have been drawn from every branch of modern culture in Europe and elsewhere. They wish to call to the attention of the Holy See, the appalling responsibility it would incur in the history of the human spirit were it to refuse to allow the Traditional Mass to survive, even though this survival took place side by side with other liturgical forms."—Ed.]

ops of the episcopal conference as to how this faculty is to be exercised will be a further guarantee of unity of praxis in this area.[51]

The indult granted to England was "criticized," as Archbishop Bugnini later acknowledged, "by part of the French episcopate and liturgical experts."[52] Conversely, groups attached to the traditional liturgy, particularly in France and in the United States, hoped that a similar indult might be granted to other countries. "But the pope was inflexible and unwilling to grant the indult to any other conference," observed Archbishop Bugnini, somewhat enigmatically adding: "The reason for this, I think, is to be found in personal considerations, in a subjective relationship between the pope and Cardinal Heenan, rather than in any rational causes of the matter."[53]

51. Letter to Cardinal Heenan from the Sacred Congregation for Divine Worship, signed A. Bugnini, 5 November 1971, Protocol number 1897/71.
52. Bugnini, *Memorie*, 85.
53. Ibid., 86.

9

Other Reforms

ONCE THE NEW Mass had been promulgated and the Congregation for Divine Worship had been created, the reform of the liturgy continued. Over the course of the years, reforms initiated years earlier came to fruition.

Liturgia Horarum

Consilium group 9 had been commissioned to prepare the reform of the Divine Office. Canon Martimort was the true conductor, leading the orchestra of subgroups that shared the work, although he was not always able to impose his own views.

The conciliar preparatory commission had made precise, sometimes bold, proposals on the reform of the breviary, especially for the reduction of the number of hours and the use of the "local language" in different cases. The conciliar Constitution had devoted an entire chapter to the Divine Office (*SC* 83–101), including nearly all of the preparatory commission's proposals and turning them into "norms" for a future revision.

It took the ninth *Consilium* group seven years of work and no less than ninety-eight reports from April 1964 to March 1970 to achieve the redaction of a new breviary, whose name itself was changed to *Liturgia Horarum* ("Liturgy of the Hours"). Bishop Isnard, a member of group 9, reported that "at first there was some hesitancy among the *Consilium* members, who as usual were split into two tendencies: the more traditionalist ones who wished to preserve all the data of Tradition, and the bolder ones who wanted a more radical reform."[1]

---

1. Isnard, "Le 'Consilium'" (see p. 87, n. 11 above), 408.

For example, Lauds and Vespers had five psalms each in the traditional breviary. At first, the attempt was made to preserve this number but, as Bishop Isnard recalled, "currents from France ended up changing the earlier vote and a total of three prevailed for those Hours." He added: "I still have the impression that Martimort would never have wanted such an abridgement of the Divine Office, but he ended up accepting it."

Another point of contention concerned the historical psalms and what are called the imprecatory psalms. Certain consultors and certain members felt that several psalms, judged too militaristic or violent, should be left out. Others, particularly Canon Martimort, deemed that the entire psalter ought to be preserved without discriminating among them according to subjective or anachronistic criteria. Bishop Spülbeck, from East Germany, one of the rare members of the *Consilium* to hail from a Communist country, put forth another reason: "Our special [i.e., political] circumstances require that the entire psalter be used. Afflicted as we are by a very difficult external situation, we need expressions suitable for use *contra diabolum*."[2]

Bugnini submitted the question to Paul VI, who answered: "It seems better to choose psalms more adapted to Christian prayer and omit the imprecatory and historical psalms (while allowing that the latter may be appropriately used on certain occasions)."[3]

During the *Consilium*'s tenth session, April 23–30, 1968, this question on the psalms was examined again. The way in which Bugnini presented the pope's opinion was probably too blunt: he considered the matter settled. Even Canon Martimort was ruffled by his manner. He was later to say: "I had thought that while the *Consilium* ought to give much consideration to the pope's wishes, it was also incumbent upon it to share its point of view with him with complete freedom."[4] Some of the participants would write to the Secretariat of State to complain that Fr Bugnini had presented "some of the pope's

---

2. Quoted in Erich Zenger, *A God of Vengeance? Understanding the Psalms of Divine Wrath* (Louisville: Westminster John Knox Press, 1996), 40.

3. Bugnini, *Reform*, 175.

4. Martimort, "Lercaro," 387.

decisions and wishes too absolutely and imperiously."[5] Yet the pope's opinion, imposed by Bugnini, prevailed: several psalms (Pss. 77, 104, and 105) were set apart for certain times of the year while three others (Pss. 57, 82, and 108) were completely suppressed.[†]

The historian Alain Besançon reacted to this self-censorship as a sociologist:

> The idea of struggle, of war, occupies such a position in the Christian Scriptures that one wonders how it can be obscured. I'm told that in the French editions of the breviary, the psalter has been expurgated of its most warlike and imprecatory scriptural verses on the grounds that they are incompatible with "modern sensibilities." This mutilation is typically Marcionite.[6]

In the reform of the Divine Office, the *Consilium* went beyond the Council's wishes. The Apostolic Constitution *Laudis Canticum* of November 1, 1970 promulgated the new Divine Office. But the four volumes of the Liturgy of the Hours only came, progressively, from July 1971 to July 1972.

The structure of the *Liturgia Horarum* is very different from that of the *Breviarium Romanum*. The principal changes may be summarized as follows:[7]

- Three of the hours (Lauds, Vespers, Compline) are considered as major and remain the fixed points of the priest's prayer life.
- The Office of Prime is suppressed and the other "little hours" (Terce, Sext, None) are reduced to a single middle hour (*ad horam mediam*), also called Midday Office.
- The Office of Matins is transformed into an Office of Readings, composed of three psalms and two readings (biblical and patristic

5. Msgr Benelli to Fr Bugnini, 8 June 1968, quoted in G. Pasqualetti, "Presentazione" in Bugnini, *Memorie*, 15.

† In addition to whole psalms, many individual verses were excised as well. For example, the famous Sunday and festal Psalm 109 (110), *Dixit Dominus,* is no longer recited in its entirety in the *Liturgia Horarum*, as verse 6 was omitted.—*Ed.*

6. Alain Besançon, *La Confusion des langues. La crise idéologique de l'Église* (Paris: Calmann-Lévy, 1978), 123–24.

7. See Stanislaus Campbell, *From Breviary to Liturgy of the Hours. The Structural Reform of the Roman Office, 1964–1971* (Collegeville: The Liturgical Press, 1995).

or hagiographical). This Office may be celebrated at any time of day.

• The recitation of the psalter is now spread over four weeks instead of one.

The Suppression of Minor Orders

The issue of minor orders provides a good illustration of the way in which bold reforms could turn out. The four minor orders (porter, lector, exorcist, acolyte) were the first degrees of Holy Orders, ahead of the three major orders (subdeacon, deacon, priest). Dom Bernard Botte had long been militating for a reform of this clerical hierarchy and the abandonment of some of the minor orders. He had brought up the matter during discussion at the preparatory commission, then drew up a daring proposal during the *Consilium*'s labors. He was presenting a general plan that provided for the suppression of several minor orders "that no longer corresponded to real usage."[8] When he presented it to Archbishop Bugnini, the latter, without opposing it, counseled caution: "Fr Bugnini let me know that, if I maintained this position, my report would go nowhere. Only one thing could be done: leave aside for a while the minor orders and begin with the major orders."

In point of fact, as time went by and other bold reforms were gaining approval, the matter could be brought up again, and Dom Botte's proposals were, in the main, adopted.

Canon Martimort reports that Paul VI wanted minor orders to be "entirely retained, but improved."[9] Yet, on August 15, 1972, he signed the motu proprio *Ministeria Quaedam* suppressing the orders of porter, exorcist, and subdeacon, as well the motu proprio *Ad Pascendum* establishing new norms for the diaconate:[10]

---

8. Dom Bernard Botte mentions this question in *From Silence to Participation* (see p. 64, n.8 above), 133.

9. A.-G. Martimort, "L'Histoire de la réforme liturgique à travers le Témoignage de Mgr Annibale Bugnini," *La Maison-Dieu* 162 (1985): 147.

10. *DOL* 340 and 319 respectively.

I. First tonsure is no longer conferred; entrance into the clerical state is joined to the diaconate.

II. What up to now were called minor orders are henceforth to be called *ministries.*

III. Ministries may be assigned to lay Christians; hence they are no longer to be considered as reserved to candidates for the sacrament of orders.

IV. Two ministries, adapted to present-day needs, are to be preserved in the whole Latin Church, namely, those of reader and acolyte. The functions heretofore assigned to the subdeacon are entrusted to the reader and the acolyte; consequently, the major order of subdiaconate no longer exists in the Latin Church.

There is no need here to go into all the details of *Ministeria Quaedam*, but it is worth noting that the ministry of lector (or "reader") is defined as follows: "The reader is appointed (*instituitur*) for a function proper to him, that of reading the Word of God in the liturgical assembly. Accordingly, he is to proclaim the readings from Sacred Scripture, except for the Gospel. . . ." It also specified, by way of prescription: "In accordance with the ancient tradition of the Church, institution to the ministries of reader and acolyte is reserved to men." In actuality, there were to be more and more (non-instituted) female readers.

Sacred Music: "My Cross to Bear"

Archbishop Bugnini would later acknowledge that "the problem of song [*del canto*] was one of the most sensitive, important, and troubling of the entire reform."[11] Before the Council, as we have seen, there had been lively discussions within the preparatory commission. The next-to-last chapter of the conciliar Constitution had been devoted to sacred music. It had given Gregorian chant a preeminent position: "The Church acknowledges Gregorian chant as specially suited to the Roman liturgy: therefore, other things being equal, it should be given pride of place in liturgical services" (*SC*

11. Bugnini, *Reform*, 885.

116). It did not, however, exclude other types of sacred music, "especially polyphony," and at the same time stated that "the people's own religious songs [*cantus popularis religiosus*] are to be encouraged with care" (*SC* 118).

As for musical instruments, while the pipe organ remained "the traditional musical instrument" that was "to be held in high esteem," other musical instruments could "be admitted for use in divine worship" if "competent territorial authority" (*SC* 120) authorized it. This was an open door.

On November 22, 1963, Paul VI had created the *Consociatio Internationalis Musicae Sacrae* ("International Association of Sacred Music"). Its mission was to inform the Holy See "of the needs of sacred music" and to promote "the cultivation of sacred music and its progress in accord with the Church's directives."[12] Whereas the Pontifical Institute of Sacred Music, whose creation went back fifty years, was the school of Gregorian tradition and sacred music in Rome and had a mission to teach, the International Association was essentially made up of representatives from the different institutes of sacred music throughout the world and of members of diocese-approved sacred music societies. It was an intermediary body between the Holy See and these institutions. It was closely linked to the Pontifical Institute since the latter's president, Msgr Higinio Anglés, was the honorary president of the *Consociatio.*

Nevertheless, the reform of sacred music was conducted not by these two institutions but by the *Consilium*, whose group 25 was set up for the "revision of chant books." This gave rise to continual conflicts. In 1965, Fr Bugnini had to leave the Pontifical Institute of Sacred Music, where he had been teaching for ten years.

Fr Pasqualetti has given a rather one-sided, black-and-white summary of the lively discussions on Gregorian chant that took place before, during, and after the Council:

> One of the major difficulties that the liturgical renewal and the participation of the people encountered came from choirmasters, especially those of the Roman basilicas, and from leaders of organizations devoted to the promotion of liturgical chant such as the

---

12. Autograph *Nobile Subsidium*, 22 November 1963; *DOL* 500.

Pontifical Institute of Sacred Music and the *Consociatio Interna-tionalis Musicae Sacrae*, for whom the only music of any value was classical, Gregorian, and polyphonic music, and who considered support for singing in the spoken language an impoverishment or even an "artistic disaster."[13]

He quotes Fr Bugnini complaining in a private communication that sacred music "remained the preparatory commission's cross to bear from the very first moment of our work, and now [it remains], like a crown, my *cross.*"

In fact, there was constant antagonism between group 25, which had the encouragement and support of Fr Bugnini, and the institutions attached to Gregorian chant and Latin in the liturgy. In May 1964, the Secretariat of State had to intervene and approach Fr Bugnini in order for the consultors to let in the choirmasters and leaders of *Scholae cantorum*. Two of the most eminent representatives of the Roman chant and sacred music tradition, Msgr Anglés, director of the Pontifical Institute of Sacred Music, and Msgr Bartolucci, choirmaster of the Sistine Chapel Choir, as well as Msgr Romita, president of the international federation *Pueri cantores*, were named consultors on June 17, 1964.

In May 1965, Msgr Anglés sent the Secretariat of State a "Prome-moria on the Impoverishment of Sacred Music" in the name of the Pontifical Institute of Sacred Music. The following month Msgr Bartolucci in turn sent it a report on "Current Problems in Sacred Music."

Fr Bugnini sought to counterbalance the influence of those defending Gregorian traditions. Thanks to his support, *Universa Laus*, the International Study Group for Liturgical Singing and Instrumental Music, was created in April 1966. It was to organize training sessions and, in the event, was destined to compete with the *Consociatio Internationalis*. The shift from "sacred music" to "liturgical singing and instrumental music" is significant. The principal *Universa Laus* organizer was Fr Joseph Gelineau, SJ, who had "invented" French-language psalm-singing already in 1947 and had composed many French liturgical songs. He was an active collabo-

13. Pasqualetti in Bugnini, *Memorie*, 57, n. 6.

rator with the Taizé ecumenical community and was a consultor at the *Consilium*.

The *Consilium*'s publications on song and sacred music were difficult to draw up. Publication of the *Graduale Simplex*, which was ready in 1965, was delayed two years because of the protests it encountered. Likewise the Instruction on Sacred Music was not published until 1967, after two years of protests and a number of rewrites. Canon Martimort reports that it was the object of "an epic battle": "Shockwaves spread from the *Consilium* to the Secretariat of State, to the Congregation of Rites. . . . There were twelve drafts in succession; finally the matter was remanded to the pope, who spent part of his summer vacation at Castelgandolfo personally working on it."[14]

Fr Bugnini was later to pass a somewhat dismissive judgment on the arguments of Msgr Anglés, Msgr Bartolucci, and Msgr Romita, deeming them "weak and at times captious."[15] Yet they did force corrections to be made, although these defenders of the Church's musical and choral traditions did not win their case in every instance.

The Instruction that came out in 1967 under the signatures of both the president of the *Consilium* and the prefect of the Congregation of Rites revealed itself in the event to be a compromise text.[16] The very notion of *sacred music* had a breadth that was not to be found in the Constitution on the Liturgy (§4b): "The term 'sacred music' here includes: Gregorian chant, the several styles of polyphony, both ancient and modern; sacred music for organ and for other permitted instruments, and the sacred, i.e., liturgical or religious, music of the people."

The entrance, offertory, and communion chants provided for in the *Graduale* may be replaced with other songs if the "competent territorial authority," i.e., the bishop, permits it (§32). While the Instruction does not rule out the use of Latin and Gregorian chant, it does limit them, in fact, to a few places, by way of concession as it were (§48): "Once the vernacular has been introduced into the Mass, local Ordinaries should determine whether it is advisable to

14. Martimort, "L'Histoire de la réforme," 140.
15. Bugnini, *Reform*, 901.
16. Instruction *Musicam sacram*, 5 March 1967, DOL 508.

retain one or more Masses in Latin, particularly sung Masses. This applies especially to great cities in churches with a large attendance of faithful using a foreign language."

This Instruction was not applied much, long being contradicted in the facts by practices that were to become entrenched.

Papal Ceremonies

Subsequently, even papal ceremonies underwent significant changes. Up until the Council, there had been a Prefecture of Pontifical Ceremonies whose prefect was Msgr Enrico Dante. Paul VI created him cardinal on February 22, 1965, without replacing him as prefect. By this time, the pope had already had Fr Jounel and Canon Martimort prepare a reform project. On February 26, 1965, a new study group was established within the *Consilium* as group 29 under the title *De ritibus Cappellae Papalis*. It numbered nine members and its relator was Fr Bugnini himself. By way of exception, its work was not subject to discussion in plenary sessions of the *Consilium*; it was presented directly to the pope. The point was, according to Archbishop Bugnini, to simplify the papal rites, especially their pomp: "The original simplicity and dignity of the altar must be restored by removing the clutter from it (*spogliandolo di quanto lo ingombra*)—candlesticks, reliquaries, miters, tiara."[17]

Then, on May 25, 1968, Paul VI established a Commission for the Prefecture of Papal Ceremonies whose purpose was "to apply the norms of the conciliar Constitution on the Liturgy to the papal ceremonies and to revise the regulations governing the prefecture itself." Fr Bugnini was appointed commissioner and was assisted by two vice-commissioners: Fr Gabrielo Brasó, former abbot of Montserrat and now president of the Benedictine congregation of Subiaco, and Msgr Virgilio Noè, consultor at the *Consilium*.

In this capacity and until 1970, Fr Bugnini directed papal ceremonies and designated the persons in charge of their preparation. Archbishop Piero Marini, who would himself later be in charge of papal ceremonies, says:

17. Bugnini, *Reform*, 806.

Msgr Bugnini profoundly reformed the papal ceremonies between 1968 and 1970. Though he never was at the pope's side himself because there was at the time a corpulent and unpleasant prelate who gave out orders in a discourteous manner, it was his responsibility to prepare the celebrations. Within a few years, the decision to turn the altar to face the people was put into practice.[18]

Also during this period, Fr Bugnini increased the Papal Choir by adding a choir to sing in Italian during some parts of the ceremonies. The choirmaster, Msgr Bartolucci, who was very attached to Gregorian chant and to Palestrina's polyphonic music, was hostile to this reform but had to give way, though not without expressing his displeasure on numerous occasions. He was to acknowledge that "Bugnini and I were on two different, and I would even say opposed, wavelengths, and we had a number of clashes. Much of the responsibility for what happened to the liturgy after the Council is his, and he often worked to promote his personal ideas."[19]

Once the new regulations for papal ceremonies had been worked out, the Office for Papal Ceremonies was created in January 1970. Fr Bugnini, who was too busy with pursuing the liturgical reform, had one of his collaborators, Msgr Virgilio Noè, named the head of this new Office.

The Protestant "Observers"

The thirteenth plenary session of the *Consilium*, which was also its last, took place April 9–10, 1970; by this time it had already been integrated into the Congregation for Divine Worship. Thirty members (nine cardinals and twenty-one bishops), thirty-two consultors, and the six "observers" attended. During this short session, drafts of the texts for the reform of the Martyrology, for the revision of the rite of Confirmation, and for a new ritual of blessings were examined.

---

18. Piero Marini, *Cérémoniaire des papes* (Paris: Bayard, 2007), 44–45.

19. Domenico Bartolucci, Interview with Wilfrid Jones, trans. Gregory Di-Pippo, *Sacred Music* 141.3 (2014): 35–40.

As usual, Paul VI greeted the participants in an audience. On this occasion, two photographs were taken: one of the whole group of participants around the pope, and the other of the pope with just the group of "observers." The two photographs were published in *Notitiae* 54 (May 1970). That showing the pope with the Protestant "observers" was reproduced in many publications, whether to illustrate the "ecumenical openness" of the liturgical reform or as proof of the "protestantization" of the Mass.[20]

The picture revealed to the public a fact that was no secret, however. The names of these "observers" were already listed in the *Consilium* directory.[21] From then on, however, there would be no end to the controversy surrounding their role in the liturgical reform, sometimes extending to claims that these "observers" had a crucial role in the elaboration of the new Missal and in the composition of certain Eucharistic Prayers. Bugnini contested that view in an article he signed with his bare initials (*ab*) and published in *Notitiae*.[22]

Vatican II had welcomed some non-Catholics from its very first session on. Their number would keep increasing. They had attended all of the Council's general congregations, but had not taken an official part in the discussions or worked in the commissions revising the *schemas*. On the other hand, they were able to express their opinions in the *extra aulam* conversations they had with bishops and *periti*, in the lectures they gave, and in the meetings to which they were invited.

The *Consilium* acted in continuity with what had been done at the Council when it included non-Catholics in its work. The first "observers" were named on August 23, 1966, over two years after the

---

20. The picture was on the front page of *Documentation catholique* of 3 May 1970. It is also found, *inter alia*, on the cover of a work criticizing the new Mass by the Brazilian theologian Arnaldo Vidigal Xavier da Silveira in its French translation, *La Nouvelle Messe de Paul VI: qu'en penser?* (Paris: Diffusion de la pensée française, 1975).

21. *Elenchus Membrorum, Consultorum, Consiliarium, Coetuum a Studiis*, 2nd ed. (Vatican City: Typis Poyglottis Vaticanis, 1967).

22. "Gli osservatori al 'Consilium,'" *Notitiae* 95–96 (July–August 1974): 249–52. Chapter 13 of Bugnini, *Reform*, 199–202, which is devoted to the subject, is essentially an expanded reprint of this article.

Consilium had begun operations. They had been picked by the institutions that they represented and their nominations had been approved by the Secretariat of State and the Congregation for the Doctrine of the Faith. The Anglican communion had delegated the Reverends Jasper and Shepherd; the World Council of Churches, Professor George; the Lutheran World Federation, Pastor Künneth; and the Taizé Community, Pastor Max Thurian. The following year a sixth "observer" was named: Reverend Brand, representing American Methodists.

These six "observers," then, had diverse origins and represented Christian communities with very different liturgical conceptions and practices. Furthermore, their small number (six Protestant observers) prevented them from playing a crucial role in the plenary sessions that numbered dozens of members and consultors.

Bugnini minimized their role:

> Their attitude at the meetings of the Consilium was one of great reserve and unobtrusiveness. They never took part in the discussions, never asked to speak. They were the first to arrive at the meetings, the last to leave the hall. They were always affable, polite, sparing of words, and ready to engage in a friendly way in any conversation that might be requested.

Yet Bugnini does point out that "only on one occasion" the views of the "observers" as a group were solicited during a plenary session: when the *schema* on the readings at Mass was under discussion. Without going into any detail, it is worth simply noting that spreading the liturgical readings over several cycles was not provided for in the conciliar Constitution.[23] Cardinal Stickler judged it to be "a sin against nature.... The yearly liturgical cycle could have stayed as it was and the enrichment of the readings still have been achieved."[24]

The way in which Bugnini presents the matter is certainly not

---

23. There are two cycles of daily readings (even and odd years) and three cycles of Sunday readings (years A, B, and C). Paul VI, on approving the *Ordo Lectionum Missae*, acknowledged that it had not been possible for him "get a complete and detailed grasp" of it. Paul VI to Bugnini, 24 June 1969, in Bugnini, *Reform*, 420.

24. Alfons Cardinal Stickler, *Témoignage d'un expert au Concile* (Paris: C.I.E.L., 2000), 52–53.

false, but it is incomplete. In addition to the private conversation he mentions, the "observers" also expressed their opinions and expectations in more regular relations with one or another member and consultor as well as through correspondence, written notes, or even papers presented to the *Consilium*. For example, Bugnini indicates that Max Thurian was consulted by group 12a, which dealt with the issue of the "universal prayer" at Mass, because Thurian's Taizé community already used this type of prayer.[25]

Bugnini at the Height of His Influence

On January 6, 1972, Fr Bugnini was named titular archbishop of Diocletiana. On the following February 13, he received the episcopal consecration from the hands of Paul VI in St. Peter's Basilica along with four other *consecrandi*.

In early 1972, Archbishop Bugnini was at the height of his power and influence. Beyond his duties as secretary of the Congregation for Divine Worship, he was also consultor at the Congregation for the Evangelization of Peoples and member of the Pontifical Central Commission for Sacred Art in Italy.

But differences in point of view and protestations against the actions of the man who was now Archbishop Bugnini would multiply and grow ever sharper. Specifically, on October 26, 1972, eight members of the International Theological Commission addressed a letter to the Congregation for Divine Worship to draw its attention to certain translations in liturgical books and to the spread of improvised Eucharistic Prayers. The International Theological Commission deplored "great dangers to the unity and integrity of the Catholic faith."[26]

25. Bugnini, *Reform*, 201, n. 3.
26. Document quoted in Bugnini, *Memorie*, 68, n. 3.

10

Fall from Grace

O N JULY 8, 1975, Archbishop Bugnini was staying at the Fiuggi spa, some 80 km southeast of Rome, when Cardinal Knox, Prefect of the Congregation for Divine Worship, came calling. He informed him under the seal of secrecy that the pope had decided to regroup the Congregation for Divine Worship and the Congregation for the Sacraments into a single dicastery. He had brought him the proofs of the Apostolic Constitution that was to make it official. Bugnini was being asked to go over the text and to point out whether there was "anything to correct." Archbishop Bugnini was convinced that he would stay on as secretary of the new Congregation.

Back in Rome, he received a telephone call from the Secretariat of State on July 14. The substitute there, Msgr Benelli, wished to see him urgently. Bugnini, after arriving in a nearly entirely deserted Rome—it was a Sunday in summer—received from the hands of Msgr Benelli a letter signed by Cardinal Villot, Secretary of State. It named him nuncio to Uruguay. The official nomination was slated for two days later, the day the creation of the new Congregation was to be announced.

Archbishop Bugnini was dumbfounded. He tried to argue: "Why, you're liquidating years of work, just like that? I don't know Spanish, I don't have the first idea in the field of diplomacy. Do you want to send me down there to die?" "Nooo!" answered Msgr Benelli, "But you're better off down there, far away; that way we won't see you anymore."[1]

---

1. Bugnini, *Memorie*, 79.

Archbishop Bugnini had "been resigned," to use his own expression. He refused his nomination to Uruguay on the grounds that he did not know Spanish, but there was nothing he could do to prevent the new Congregation from being established. He had to vacate his office on August 1.

Bugnini's Opponents

Archbishop Bugnini would say that he never exactly knew the reason for his sudden dismissal even though he "knocked on many doors at all levels."[2] In reality, he had been running into opposition throughout his career at the *Consilium* and then at the Congregation for Divine Worship. His adversaries, then and later, deplored his great influence on Paul VI and denounced his omnipotence. In his own lengthy book on the liturgical reform, he stresses the close collaboration he shared with Paul VI over the course of eleven years, and in his memoirs he underscores the trust he enjoyed (until 1975): "he had asked me for advice every time there was a change in the Congregation, often on matters of detail."[3]

His sudden fall from grace was incomprehensible to him. He wrote to Paul VI several times to ask for explanations. He never received an answer. The pope called him in one day in July through his secretary, by way of leavetaking and thanks. Paul VI gave Archbishop Bugnini an *editio princeps* of the Gelasian Sacramentary, a facsimile of a manuscript kept at the Vatican library. Of this meeting, Archbishop Bugnini says: "But I was so mortified and despondent that I did not have the strength to say much. He was more mortified than I was."[4]

At different points in his autobiographical memoirs Archbishop Bugnini casts about for an explanation to his eviction: "I only ever found it in court intrigues, in the open sworn enmity of Cardinal Seper and of the sub-secretary, Msgr Noè, and in the gratuitous

---

2. Id., *Reform*, 90.
3. Id., *Memorie*, 81.
4. Ibid.

Fall from Grace

accusation from the enemies of the reform that I belonged to Free-masonry."[5]

It is surprising to find the name of Msgr Virgilio Noè among the hostile prelates. Msgr Noè, sub-secretary at the Congregation for Divine Worship at the time, had been Bugnini's principal collaborator. In his subsequent career, he came to be noted as an eminent representative of the "Bugnini school." Their differences of opinion remain to be examined.

On the other hand, it is not surprising to find Cardinal Seper's name mentioned. As Prefect of the Congregation for the Doctrine of the Faith since January 1968, Cardinal Seper had always proven to be anxious to defend the integrity of the faith, including in liturgical matters. He was one of the cardinals who had been critical of the new *Ordo Missae*. As he was examining the second Eucharistic Prayer, which in his view lent itself to dubious interpretations, he had told his confrere Cardinal Oddi: "Me? I'll never adopt that Canon."[6]

The last opposition between Cardinal Seper and Archbishop Bugnini bore on the Eucharistic Prayers composed in Belgium and in the Netherlands. Canon Martimort himself, usually so favorably disposed to Archbishop Bugnini's work, acknowledged that "the worst failure of the Congregation for Divine Worship was without question its Eucharistic Prayer project" and that at the time Archbishop Bugnini relied on collaborators "who did not always have the theological maturity and pastoral sense required by the issues at hand."[7]

In the period immediately following the Council and in the early 1970s, Belgium and the Netherlands went through a turbulent time in pastoral (the "pastoral Council" of Holland), doctrinal (the notorious *Dutch Catechism*), and liturgical terms. Not content with the four Eucharistic Prayers contained in the new *Ordo* of the Mass, the Churches of the Netherlands and Belgium composed new Eucharistic Prayers. Five of them were authorized for experimentation in

5. Ibid.
6. Quoted by Cardinal Oddi, Interview, *Trente Jours* (July–August 1991): 15.
7. Martimort, "L'Histoire," 154.

1969.[8] In 1975, the bishops of Belgium asked for the authorization to use these Eucharistic Prayers to be confirmed definitively. Archbishop Bugnini took advantage of this request to submit more Eucharistic Prayers as well: three for Masses for children and two for "reconciliation" Masses.[9]

Paul VI, to whom Archbishop Bugnini presented the request, wanted the texts to be examined by a mixed commission composed of consultors from the Congregation for Divine Worship and consultors from the Congregation for the Discipline of the Sacraments. At the same time, April 22, 1975, the Secretariat of State sent Archbishop Bugnini a stern letter restating the procedure to follow for the examination and approval of requests sent in by bishops' conferences.[10] The commission's first meeting, on May 21, 1975, asked for a "radical revision of the texts," as Archbishop Bugnini acknowledges. Then, on the following June 19, a mixed ordinary congregation took place, including representatives of the Congregation for the Doctrine of the Faith, Cardinal Seper in particular. He expressed his total opposition to granting any new Eucharistic Prayers as he judged that this would open the door to an endless multiplication of anaphoras. Nevertheless, Archbishop Bugnini did thereafter obtain an approval from Paul VI for the new Eucharistic Prayers "in view of the pastoral arguments" he had been presented with.

A severe blow had been dealt to the authority of the prefect of the Congregation for the Doctrine of the Faith and to the majority opinion of the mixed ordinary congregation. Cardinal Seper may have demanded from the pope Archbishop Bugnini's departure.[11] Lastly, at the very moment that Archbishop Bugnini was dismissed, *Notitiae*, the journal of the Congregation for Divine Worship, published a very severe warning (the title was "Aberrations") against two collections of Eucharistic Prayers published by Jesuit authors in

8. Bugnini, *Reform*, 483–84.

9. Marini, 147.

10. Bugnini himself had the honesty of quoting this letter in full, *Reform*, 481.

11. The well-known Italian daily *Il Tempo* of 12 September 1975 published an article under the title "Revolt of 19 Cardinals at the Vatican Against a Powerful Monsignore" ("Rivolta di 19 cardinali in Vaticano contro un potente monsignore"), cited in Marini, 149–50, n. 57.

the United States and in Italy: "Sometimes even the words of Consecration are altered. One using them would certainly not be performing the rite instituted by the Lord."[12]

Freemason?

Just a few months after his dismissal, Archbishop Bugnini started being accused of having belonged to Freemasonry. This rumor first spread *sotto voce*, then became public in the press, and is repeated to this day. Nevertheless, it was not the determining factor in Bugnini's dismissal; it is rather a later element added to other, older, criticisms directed at his work in the liturgical reform.

Archbishop Bugnini tells the story of how he came to hear of this accusation.[13] It was sometime after his dismissal from the Congregation for Divine Worship, in the summer of 1975. Don Gino Belleri, a priest who acted as Cardinal Oddi's secretary, informed him of the rumor that was spreading at the Vatican and that reportedly rested on reliable sources. He had the information from Cardinal Oddi himself. Archbishop Bugnini wanted to know more. Cardinal Oddi agreed to come and see him and told him "word for word" that he had seen his actual signature on a document proving membership in Freemasonry and that he knew from a reliable source that Freemasonry paid him half a million liras per month. "This revelation did not bother me," Archbishop Bugnini later reported. "I was so sure of myself that I gave him the firmest of denials." Nevertheless, he wished to defend himself before Paul VI. In October of 1975, he wrote him a letter which, however, remained unanswered.

The accusation was first publicized in the press a few months later, in the spring of 1976. A little research allows for the reconstruction of the chronology of this public accusation:

• Archbishop Lefebvre was the first to mention the rumor in public. Perhaps Cardinal Oddi or writer Tito Casini informed him? He wrote in the tenth issue of his *Newsletter to Friends and Benefactors* (27 March 1976):

12. "Aberrazioni," *Notitiae* 11 (June–July 1975): 169.
13. Bugnini, *Memorie*, 94–97.

When one learns in Rome that the man who was the soul of the liturgical reform was a Freemason, one may well think that he was not alone. The veil masking the greatest deception ever to target clergy and laity is doubtless starting to tear. Now more than ever, therefore, we must remain faithful to Tradition, to the perennial Church, and pray God, the Most Holy Virgin, and Saint Michael the Archangel to deliver the Church from the scandalous occupation of which she is the victim.

• The following month, Tito Casini, on the last page of his new work *Nel Fumo di Satana*,[14] in a clause that seems added at the last minute, speaks of the liturgical reform "conducted by a Bugnini who finally revealed himself to be what we suspected: a Freemason."

• Yet another month later, Jean Madiran repeated the accusation on the front page of the *Supplément-voltigeur*, the supplement to his review *Itinéraires*: "At the Vatican, the principal mover until 1975 was a Freemason."[15] Jean Madiran relies entirely on Archbishop Lefebvre's and Tito Casini's accusations.

• Next came Italian traditionalist journals: Luigi Villa's *Chiesa Viva* and Don Francesco Putti's *Sì sì No no* in June 1976.

When the major Italian newspapers took hold of the story beginning in the summer of 1976 (a year after Archbishop Bugnini's dismissal, therefore), the articles would apparently be better and better documented and provide the precise date of Archbishop Bugnini's alleged entrance into Freemasonry, his initiation number, and his pseudonym. Then followed longer and longer lists of supposed Freemasonic cardinals and prelates.

Archbishop Bugnini himself was far from Rome, having been at his post in Tehran for a few months already. He wrote to Paul VI a new and lengthy letter containing an absolute denial of his "presumed membership in Freemasonry": "I must firmly state what I was in a position to write to Your Holiness last October: that I NEVER, whether directly or indirectly, whether in act or by formal

---

14. Tito Casini, *Nel Fumo di Satana* (Florence: Il Carro di San Giovanni, 1976), 150.

15. *Supplément-voltigeur* 38 (15 May 1976).

membership, have been a part of Masonry, or of any other group or movement that approaches or resembles it."[16]

This new letter went unanswered. Sometime later, for the first and only time, Archbishop Bugnini would publicly defend himself against this accusation. Rather than through an interview or an article, he did so by having a declaration published in a confidential religious newsletter published in France by the Knights of Our Lady, *Magistère-information*. This publication had links to certain traditional circles at the Vatican and in France. The short declaration stated: "Archbishop A. Bugnini leaves his defense up to the Holy See if it deems it useful; but he categorically denies ever having had the slightest contact in any way with Freemasonry or any other society of the sort."[17]

Naturally, Archbishop Bugnini knew that the major newspapers would pick up this declaration, which is just what occurred. The following October 8, *Le Figaro* published an article under the title "Archbishop Bugnini: 'I am not a Freemason.'" It republished the declaration above. Jean Bourdarias, who wrote the article, added: "To have written these lines, Archbishop Bugnini, whom some seem to blame for being overly discreet, must have been deeply wounded and bruised by a course of action that will, in the final analysis, turn against those who have adopted it."

Two days later, October 10, 1976, *L'Osservatore Romano* published a critical note by its vice director, Msgr Virgilio Levi, against *Sì sì No no*; it stated regarding the lists that the press had been publishing: "None of the Vatican prelates (*prelati vaticani*) mentioned has ever had any dealings with Freemasonry."

The accusation of belonging to Freemasonry did not stop there. Yet the documents published in the press at the time (matriculation number lists, etc.) are inconclusive and do not resist historical criticism (documentary authenticity, sourcing, etc.). In 2012, I was able to interview Fr Carlo Braga, one of Archbishop Bugnini's closest collaborators for decades, on this supposed membership in Freemasonry. He revealed to me that he had asked the question himself,

---

16. Bugnini to Paul VI, 19 July 1976, in *Memorie*, 100–102.
17. *Magistère-information* 144 (1 October 1976): 2.

point blank. Archbishop Bugnini answered: "I would never have taken that step."

Whatever the case may be, this accusation of belonging to Freemasonry was not the determining factor in Archbishop Bugnini's dismissal. As we have seen, there was opposition from the Congregation for the Doctrine of the Faith, from the International Theological Commission, and from the Secretariat of State. Archbishop Marini, one of Archbishop Bugnini's close collaborators until the latter's dismissal, was later to speak of the Roman Congregations' "overreaction" to Bugnini's "singlemindedness, even stubbornness."[18]

There is also the fact that Paul VI "progressively withdrew" his trust from Archbishop Bugnini, as Fr Gy, who knew both men quite well, pointed out no less than thirty years ago. He also noticed, "from 1972 or 1973 on, signs of a change in Paul VI's attitude—not in his attitude towards the liturgical reform, which was his own, but in his way of looking at the postconciliar situation and at Bugnini's grasp of it. Did the latter notice?"[19]

+ + +

Translator's note: The author states (on the preceding page) that Archbishop Bugnini defended himself only once against the accusation of belonging to Freemasonry. This holds true for Europe, but Bugnini was led to defend himself once in an American review as well. These are the events that led to this second instance:

- A Rev. Robert G. Keating of Derby, Connecticut, wrote a letter to the editor of the *Homiletic and Pastoral Review* on the topic of communion in the hand in which he repeated Tito Casini's claim of Bugnini's membership in Freemasonry ("Fraught with Danger," *HPR* 79.4 [January 1979]: 6–7). He had read Casini's allegation in Michael Davies, *Liturgical Revolution*, vol. 2, *Pope John's Council* (New Rochelle, NY, Arlington House, 1977), 166.

18. Marini, 157.
19. P.-M. Gy, "Mgr Bugnini et la réforme liturgique de Vatican II," *Revue des sciences philosophiques et théologiques* 69 (April 1985): 316.

• Fr Charles E. Miller of St. John's Seminary in Camarillo, California, a Vincentian like Archbishop Bugnini, responded in a letter to the editor of the same review to defend his confrere, stating that to "label him a Freemason is an objective calumny" and demanding an apology ("Communion in the Hand," *HPR* 79.10 [July 1979]: 5–6).

• Michael Davies in turn wrote a letter to the editor to respond to Fr Miller. He reported that a "Roman priest of the very highest standing came into the possession of evidence which, he considered, proved the Archbishop to be a Mason. This evidence was placed into the hands of Pope Paul VI who abolished the Congregation for Divine Worship ... and banished the Archbishop to Iran as Pro-Nuncio" ("On Opposing Communion in the Hand," *HPR* 80.4 [January 1980]: 6–8). Davies, however, explicitly refrained from claiming that this proved Bugnini's membership in Freemasonry; he wrote only that it proved that the evidence convinced Paul VI of the accusation.

• At this point, in the spring of 1980, Archbishop Bugnini wrote a letter to the editor of the *Homiletic and Pastoral Review*. In it he quotes the denial published in *Le Figaro* on 8 October 1976, adding: "for him [Davies] and his colleagues, calumniators by profession ... I repeat what I wrote in 1976: 'I do not own anything in this world more precious than the pectoral cross: if one is able to prove, honestly and objectively, an iota of truth of what they affirm, I am ready to return back the pectoral cross'" ("Archbishop A. Bugnini Denies Freemason Connection," *HPR* 80.8 [May 1980]: 4–6).

• The exchange ended with a last letter from Davies, who quoted (in Italian) from the letter he had received in the meantime from the Roman priest claiming to have seen the evidence of Bugnini's membership in Freemasonry and to have put it into Paul VI's hands ("Michael T. Davies Replies to Archbishop Bugnini," *HPR* 81.1 [October 1980]: 4–6). Davies would go on to outline his case in the third volume of his *Liturgical Revolution: Pope Paul's New Mass* (Kansas City, MO: Angelus Press, 1990), 504–10.

11

Apostolic Nuncio in Iran

A s soon as he was dismissed, Archbishop Bugnini decided to tell the history of the liturgical reform, even though it was not yet complete. He said it was "two-thirds" complete. Specifically, the new Book of Blessings, the Ceremonial of Bishops, and the Martyrology were missing.

Although he was not its sole instigator, Archbishop Bugnini had directed the liturgical reform since the end of 1963, close to twelve years in all. He had started to work on this history by July 1975. It was a work both of self-justification and of memorialization. It quotes numerous original documents and took six years to write.

Meanwhile, he had been sent to Iran as nuncio. The Secretariat of State and the pope had been patient after his refusal to go to Uruguay. Then, a few months later, early in December, another posting was proposed to him, now in Iran where the diplomatic language was French. This time Archbishop Bugnini deemed the posting impossible to refuse, particularly since the Congregation of Missions had ancient ties to the country. The Vincentians had had many institutions there for years. The apostolic delegation to Persia, created in 1874, had first had a Vincentian at its head. Also, as we have seen, Bishop Alcide Giuseppe Marina, who had ordained Bugnini to the priesthood, then had left for Persia where he was Apostolic Delegate from 1936 to 1945.

Archbishop Bugnini's nomination as apostolic nuncio to Tehran was published on January 5, 1976. On January 6, he sent a long, typewritten letter to all his friends and to those who had worked with him at the *Consilium* and at the Congregation for Divine Worship to announce his departure and to thank them for their collaboration. Without openly mentioning his dismissal, he did justify himself in veiled terms: "At a great moment of her history, we have endeavored to serve the Church, not to use her." In the letter addressed to Dom Adalbert Franquesa, his dear friend at the Abbey of Montserrat, he added a few handwritten lines: "Oh! how rare *true* friends are! We added 'Ubi caritas est *vera*' in the famous hymn but oh! how rare it is in the Church. I hope to find more of it among the Muslims...."[1]

He arrived in Tehran on February 3. He stayed at his post until his death in 1982, with a few temporary returns to Rome.

The "Lefebvre Case"

A few months after Archbishop Bugnini's arrival in Tehran, severe canonical sanctions were taken against Archbishop Lefebvre. There is no need here to go over the steps leading up to the condemnation of the founder of the Society of Saint Pius X and of the seminary at Écône. On June 12, 1976, Msgr Benelli, substitute at the Secretariat of State, "by special mandate of the Sovereign Pontiff," communicated to Archbishop Lefebvre that "in the current state of affairs and pursuant to the provisions of canon 2373, §1 of the Code of Canon Law," he was to "refrain rigorously" from proceeding to the priestly ordinations slated for the following June 29.

Once Archbishop Lefebvre had disregarded this prohibition, Cardinal Baggio, prefect of the Congregation of Bishops, sent him a canonical monition in the pope's name on July 6, which urged him "to change his attitude, humbly to ask forgiveness of the Holy Father, and to repair the spiritual harm that had been inflicted upon the recently ordained young priests and the scandal caused to the People of God" within ten days. Archbishop Lefebvre answered on July 17 in a letter that was not deemed "satisfactory" and which "deeply pained" the pope.

On July 22, therefore, the same Congregation for Bishops communicated to Archbishop Lefebvre its decision to penalize him with "the suspension *a divinis* provided for by canon 2279 §2.2."

1. Archbishop Bugnini to Dom Adalbert Franquesa, 6 January 1976 (archives of the Abbey of Montserrat).

And so by early July, before this last sanction, Cardinal Villot, the Secretary of State, had sent to all Holy See diplomatic representatives in the world "abundant documentation on the Lefebvre case."[2] Once he had made himself familiar with the documentation, Archbishop Bugnini wrote to Cardinal Villot (the suspension had not yet been pronounced): "I am convinced that while His Excellency Archbishop Lefebvre is stubborn in his ideas, his collaborators are more poisonous (*velenosi*)." Archbishop Bugnini made the following suggestion: "Even in this extreme case I would continue with the weapons of exhortation, of patience, of charity, and of prayer that the Holy Father has been using so far. In my humble opinion, one must at all costs avoid a break from which it would be far more difficult to return."[3] But the canonical sanction against Archbishop Lefebvre had already been decided; it was announced on July 22.

The following September, Archbishop Bugnini received a visit from Cardinal Pignedoli who stopped over in Tehran on his way to Japan. He made this stop in Tehran out of friendship for Archbishop Bugnini, but also—although he did not explicitly tell him as much—at Paul VI's suggestion: the pope wished to send a friendly signal to the man he had had to remove a year earlier.[4]

In the conversations he had with Cardinal Pignedoli, Archbishop Bugnini mentioned the liturgical situation and the "Lefebvre case." Archbishop Bugnini suggested that some kind of agreement ought to be found with Archbishop Lefebvre to calm the situation. Cardinal Pignedoli encouraged him to communicate his suggestion to Rome, and Archbishop Bugnini sent a second letter to Cardinal Villot.[5] He suggested that the celebration of the traditional Mass might once again be authorized, on condition that Archbishop Lefebvre agree to certain commitments. Archbishop Bugnini listed four such commitments:

---

2. Such is Bugnini's expression, *Memorie*, 86.
3. Bugnini to Villot, 21 July 1976, ibid.
4. In an audience in Rome on March 7, 1977, Paul VI would say to Archbishop Bugnini: "You did see that I even sent you Cardinal Pignedoli?" Ibid., 103.
5. Bugnini to Villot, 21 September 1976, ibid., 88–90.

1. A declaration that the "new" Mass is not heretical or Protestant, and that those who composed and approved it are not heretics and Protestants.

2. The *Ordo Missae* may be that of the old Missal (1962), but the readings are to be made according to their new ordering, in the vernacular, and from the ambo facing the people.

3. The Mass of St. Pius V shall be celebrated in specifically determined churches and on a fixed schedule, or for those groups who have difficulty in adapting to the new "Ordo."

4. The implementation of these dispositions is to be entrusted to the pastoral care of the local Ordinary.

Archbishop Bugnini's proposal was submitted to Paul VI, who judged it inopportune. In his answer to Archbishop Bugnini, Cardinal Villot wrote: "[The Holy Father] has asked me to communicate to you that it has not seemed opportune to grant now what has been denied in the past, and also not to worsen the confusion and disorientation by undermining the credibility of the Holy See."[6]

The door that Paul VI closed would be reopened by John Paul II (1984 indult and 1988 motu proprio) and, to a greater degree yet, by Benedict XVI (2007 motu proprio); both popes progressively gave back to the traditional Mass its "citizenship" in the Church.

The Iranian Revolution

Archbishop Bugnini devotes one of the four chapters in his *Memorie autobiografiche* to describing his work as apostolic nuncio in Iran, his relations with the different Christian communities present in that country, with the political authorities and the Shiite clergy, and his travels in neighboring countries. He took a keen interest in the history of Catholicism in the country where he represented the Holy See and would write a book 471 pages long on the history of the Catholic Church in Iran.[7]

---

6. Villot to Bugnini, 4 October 1976, ibid., 90.
7. A. Bugnini, *La Chiesa in Iran* (Rome: Centro Liturgico Vincenziano–Edizioni Vincenziane, 1981).

He was posted in Tehran when the Iranian revolution broke out; it soon became an Islamic revolution.[8] From 1977 on, criticisms had been developing against the regime of the Shah of Iran, Mohammed Reza Pahlavi. Jimmy Carter, a passionate defender of human rights, had encouraged them.

Protest letters, meetings, and demonstrations demanded the strict application of the Iranian Constitution and the respect of public liberties. From the end of 1977 on, the Shiite clergy and Ayatollah Khomeini, who was in exile at the time, also began to oppose the imperial regime, deeming it decadent and denouncing it as a vassal of the West and its false values. On January 9, 1978, a large demonstration was put down in the town of Qom, one of Shiite Islam's holy cities; this led to a cycle of massive and violent demonstrations reaching all the larger urban areas and shaking the whole country for months on end. The demonstrations in late 1978 were the most impressive in their size and their violent rejection of the existing regime. Archbishop Bugnini expressed his empathy for the demonstrators in a letter to a friend:

> We are so glad. These people had for centuries been "coerced," "oppressed." Now that they've been able to vent their frustration for eight hours straight: *Abbasso* ["down with…"], *Eviva* ["long live…"], *A morte* ["death to…"], now they are happy. Yesterday, today, they were relaxed, joyful, as if now everything can be fixed. How true it is that everyone loves freedom![9]

On January 16, 1979, the Shah of Iran left his country. On February 1, Ayatollah Khomeini returned from exile and imposed himself as leader of the revolution in a matter of months. In March, the Islamic Republic of Iran was established by referendum.

In his memoirs, Archbishop Bugnini devotes only a short paragraph to the Islamic revolution, in which he speaks only of an "incandescent and messy time."[10] His actual reactions and possible

---

8. Michael Axworthy, *Revolutionary Iran: A History of the Islamic Republic* (New York: Oxford University Press, 2013).

9. Bugnini to Dom Adalbert Franquesa, Christmas 1978, Montserrat Abbey archives.

10. Id., *Memorie*, 162.

initiatives will only be available for assessment once his correspondence with the Holy See at the Vatican archives is opened up for research.

Four Books

Archbishop Bugnini wrote a good deal while posted in Tehran. He wrote the work on the Church in Iran mentioned above. He also wrote his *Memorie autobiografiche*, a work he completed on July 19, 1977. Archbishop Bugnini entrusted the manuscript to his secretary, Fr Pasqualetti, as a "testament." It would not be published until a long time later, on the occasion of Archbishop Bugnini's posthumous 100th birthday in 2012.

We have seen that as soon as he was dismissed in 1975, Archbishop Bugnini started writing the history of the liturgical reform he had headed. He wrote this work both as documentation and as self-justification; to do so, he did not hesitate to publish documents and letters that should have remained in the archives of the Congregation he was leaving. He finished the work on August 6, 1981, the third anniversary of Paul VI's death. He wanted to render a "grateful homage" to the pope who had been the "true leader of the liturgical reform." The book, *La Riforma liturgica*, only came out two years later, after Bugnini's death.

On the other hand, in 1981 Archbishop Bugnini was able to publish an anthology of Saint Vincent de Paul's writings and a collection of his thoughts for the fourth centenary of the saint's birthday.[11]

In April 1982, for Easter, Archbishop Bugnini wrote to Cardinal Casaroli, Secretary of State, to ask him to be relieved of his diplomatic mission in Tehran. He was close to seventy years old and wished to resume pastoral duties in the Congregation of the Mission in Italy. In answer, he was told that the pope wished him to remain posted in Tehran in consideration of the delicate situation in Iran and his knowledge of the country.

Health problems compelled him to return to Rome a few months

---

11. A. Bugnini, *San Vincenzo de Paul. Pensieri* (Rome: Edizione Vincenziane, 1981).

later to undergo surgery at the Pio XI clinic. There he died of an embolism on July 3, 1982.

Four days later, his faithful disciple, Fr Pasqualetti, wrote to their common friend Dom Adalbert Franquesa: "His body now rests in his home village's cemetery. On the tombstone, the epitaph he wanted summarizes the ideal that dominated his existence: *Liturgiae amator et cultor.*"[12]

Did Archbishop Bugnini truly "love" and "serve" the liturgy? Or did he, by dint of his conception of the liturgy—true liturgy has to be "parochial" and "dynamic"[13]—and of his constructivist will, contribute to its "disintegration"? This last expression is Cardinal Ratzinger's in 1997. The future Benedict XVI did not explicitly name Archbishop Bugnini, but he questioned the break introduced by the "new Mass": "But I was dismayed by the prohibition of the old missal, since nothing of the sort had ever happened in the entire history of the liturgy." He also incriminated the manner in which this "new Mass" had been put together:

> Pius V had simply ordered a reworking of the *Missale Romanum* then being used, which is the normal thing as history develops over the course of the centuries . . . it was a continual process of growth and purification in which continuity was never destroyed. . . . There is no such thing as a "Missal of Pius V," created by Pius V himself. There is only the reworking done by Pius V as one phase in a long history of growth.

On the other hand, the liturgical reform enacted after Vatican II made "the liturgy appear to be no longer a living development but the product of erudite work and juridical authority; this has caused us enormous harm."[14]

---

12. Gottardo Pasqualetti to Adalbert Franquesa, 7 July 1982, Montserrat Abbey archives.

13. A. Bugnini, "La comunità e il rinnovamento liturgico attuale," *Annali della Missione* 69.6 (1962), 535: "The liturgy is essentially parochial, i.e., has its fullness and perfection in the parish and feeds on the spirit of the parish. The faithful cannot fully live the liturgy in a cathedral or an abbey, or in a shrine or a *rettoria* [a seminary or religious institute's chapel], but only in a parish."

14. Joseph Ratzinger, *Milestones: Memoirs, 1927–1977* (San Francisco: Ignatius, 1998), 148, 146.

Sources and Bibliography

Archives

Archives of the Congregation of the Mission (Paris): articles and works by A. Bugnini.

Archives of Montserrat Abbey (Spain): letter from A. Bugnini to Dom Adalbert Franquesa.

Archives of the *Association des Amis du cardinal Tisserant* (Montferrer, France): letter of A. Bugnini to Cardinal Tisserant.

Interview with Fr Carlo Braga (1927–2014) in Rome, 15 October 2012, and correspondence.

Print Sources

Acta Apostolicae Sedis. Vatican City: Typis Polyglottis Vaticanis, 1909–.

Annuario Pontificio. Vatican City: Typis Polyglottis Vaticanis, 1912–.

Barba, Maurizio. *Institutio Generalis Missalis Romani. Textus, Synopsis, Variationes*. Vatican City: Libreria Editrice Vaticana, 2006.

Braga, Carlo. *La Riforma liturgica di Pio XII. Documenti*. Vol. 1, *La "Memoria sulla riforma liturgica."* Rome: Centro Liturgico Vincenziano–Edizioni Liturgiche, 2003.

La Documentation catholique. Paris: Bayard, 1919–.

Lameri, Angelo. *La "Pontificia Commissio de sacra liturgia praeparatoria Concilii Vaticani II." Documenti, Testi, Verbali*. Rome: Centro Liturgico Vincenziano–Edizioni Liturgiche, 2013.

Notitiae: Commentarii ad nuntia de re liturgica, Vatican: Libreria Editrice Vaticana, 1965–.

Monographs and Articles by Archbishop Bugnini

Il Sign. Rocco Petrone, C.M. (1868–1942). Testimonianze e ricordi. Rome: Edizioni Liturgiche e Missionarie, 1942.

"La comunità e il rinnovamento liturgico attuale." *Annali della Missione* 69.6 (1962): 345–58.

La Nostra Missa. Rome: Edizioni Liturgiche, 1949.

La Riforma liturgica (1948–1975). Rome: Centro Liturgico Vincenziano–Edizioni Liturgiche, 1983. Revised edition, 1997. Eng. ed.: *The Reform of the Liturgy (1948–1975).* Trans. Matthew J. O'Connell. Collegeville, MN: Liturgical Press, 1990.

"Liturgiae cultor et amator, servi la Chiesà." Memorie autobiografiche. Rome: Centro Liturgico Vincenziano–Edizioni Liturgiche, 2012.

"Manuali italiani di liturgia." *Ephemerides Liturgicae* 59 (1945): 334–44.

"Per una riforma liturgica generale." *Ephemerides Liturgicae* 63 (1949): 406–30.

"Una particolarità del Messale da rivedere: la preghiera 'Pro iudaei' al Venerdì Santo." In *Miscellanea Giulio Belvederi*, 117–32. Vatican City: Pontificio Istituto di Archeologia Cristiana, 1954.

"Verso una riforma del Martyrologium romanum?" *Ephemerides Liturgicae* 61 (1947): 91–97.

Monographs and Articles on Archbishop Bugnini, the Liturgical Movement, and the Liturgical Reform

Bedeschi, Lorenzo. *Il Cardinale destituito. Documento sul "caso" Lercaro.* Turin: Gribaudi, 1968.

Belœil, Dominique. "Le vin dans la liturgie catholique aujourd'hui. La restauration de la communion des fidèles au calice depuis le concile Vatican II après plusieurs siècles de disparition." In *Le corps, le vin et les images*, ed. H. Cahuzac et M. Joly, 87–96. Paris: L'Harmattan, 2005.

Botte, Bernard. *From Silence to Participation. An Insider's View of Renewal.* Trans. John Sullivan. Washington, DC: Pastoral Press, 1988.

Bouyer, Louis. *The Memoirs of Louis Bouyer: From Youth and Conversion to Vatican II, the Liturgical Reform, and After.* Trans. John Pepino. Kettering, OH: Angelico Press, 2015.

Braga, Carlo. "Ricordo di Mons. Annibale Bugnini." *Notitiae* 193–94 (1982): 441–52.

_____. "La Preparazione della Costituzione 'Sacrosanctum

Concilium." In *Mens concordat voci. Mélanges offerts à Mgr A.-G. Martimort*, 381–403. Paris: Desclée, 1983.

————. "Il Centro di Azione Liturgica a servizio del Movimento liturgico." In *50 anni alla luce del Movimento liturgico*, ed. Luca Brandolini, 45–64. Rome: Centro Liturgico Vincenziano–Edizioni Liturgiche, 1998.

Campbell, Stanislaus. *From Breviary to Liturgy of the Hours. The Structural Reform of the Roman Office, 1964–1971*. Collegeville, MN: The Liturgical Press, 1995.

Casini, Tito. *The Torn Tunic: Letter of a Catholic on the "Liturgical Reform."* Trans. anon. Rome: Fidelity Books, 1967.

Cavaterra, Emilio. *Il Prefetto del Sant'Offizio. Le opere e i giorni del cardinale Ottaviani*. Milan: Editore Mursia, 1990.

Derville, Guillaume. *La concélébration eucharistique. Du symbole à la réalité*. Montreal: Wilson & Lafleur, 2011.

Dubois, Jacques. "Les saints du nouveau calendrier. Tradition et critique historiques." *La Maison-Dieu* 100 (1969): 157–78.

Duployé, Pie. *Les Origines du Centre de Pastorale Liturgique*. Mulhouse: Salvator, 1968.

Evenou, Jean. "Le 40e anniversaire de la fondation du Centre de Pastorale Liturgique (13 décembre 1943)." *La Maison-Dieu* 57 (1984): 7–14.

Faggioli, Massimo. *Vera riforma. Liturgia ed ecclesiologia nel Vaticano II*. Bologna: EDB, 2013. Eng. ed.: *True Reform: Liturgy and Ecclesiology in* Sacrosanctum Concilium. Collegeville, MN: Liturgical Press, 2012.

Fappani, Antonio. *Padre Giulio Bevilacqua, il cardinale parocco*. Brescia: Editrice Queriniana, 1979.

Geffroy, Christophe. *Benoît XVI et "la paix liturgique."* Paris: Cerf, 2008.

Giampietro, Nicolas. *The Development of the Liturgical Reform As Seen by Cardinal Ferdinando Antonelli from 1948 to 1970*. Fort Collins, CO: Roman Catholic Books, 2009.

Gy, Pierre-Marie. "L'œuvre scientifique de Dom Bernard Botte." *La Maison-Dieu* 114 (1973): 141–46.

————. "L'œuvre scientifique de Josef Andreas Jungmann." *La Maison-Dieu* 121 (1975): 159–65.

————. "Mgr Bugnini et la réforme liturgique de Vatican II."

Revue des sciences philosophiques et théologiques 69 (April 1985): 314–19.

Haquin, André. "La réforme liturgique de Vatican II. Bilan de vingt années et tâches actuelles." *Nouvelle Revue Théologique* 107.4 (1985): 481–97.

Isnard, Clemente José Carlos. "Le 'Consilium'." In *Mirabile laus canticum. Mélanges liturgiques, études historiques, portraits de liturgistes*. Ed. A.-G. Marimort. Rome: Centro Liturgico Vincenziano–Edizioni Liturgiche, 1991.

Jounel, Pierre. "Les sources françaises du missel de Paul VI." *Questions liturgiques* 52 (1971): 310–14.

————. R. Kaczynski, and G. Pasqualetti. *Liturgia opera divina e umana. Studi sulla riforma liturgica offerti a S. E. Mons. Annibale Bugnini in occasione del suo 70ᵉ compleanno*. Rome: Centro Liturgico Vincenziano–Edizioni Liturgiche, 1982.

————. "Genèse et théologie de la Constitution *Sacrosanctum Concilium*." *La Maison-Dieu* 155 (1983): 7–29.

Madiran, Jean. *Sur la lettre du cardinal Ottaviani à Paul VI*. Supplement to *Itinéraires* 142 (April 1970).

Marini, Piero. "Elenco degli '*Schemas*' del 'Consilium' e della Congregazione per il Culto divino." *Notitiae* 195–96 (October–November 1982): 453–772.

————. *A Challenging Reform. Realizing the Vision of the Liturgical Renewal*. Collegeville, MN: Liturgical Press, 2007.

————. *Cérémoniaire des papes*. Paris: Bayard, 2007.

Martimort, Aimé-Georges. "Dom Lambert Beauduin et le Centre de Pastorale Liturgique." *Questions liturgiques et paroissiales* 40 (1959): 243–51.

————. "Dom Bernard Capelle abbé du Mont César (1894–1961)." *La Maison-Dieu* 68 (1961): 203–07.

————. "Mgr Raoul Harscouët (1874–1954) et le renouveau liturgique." *Notre-Dame de Chartres* 21 (1974): 5–9 and 22 (1975): 4–7.

————. "Padre Giulio Bevilacqua e la riforma liturgica conciliare." In *L'impegno religioso e civile di P. Giulio Bevilacqua*, ed. Carlo Manziana, 85–93. Brescia: CEDOC, 1983.

————. "Du Centre de Pastorale Liturgique à la constitution liturgique de Vatican II." *La Maison-Dieu* 157 (1984): 15–31.

_____. "La Constitution sur la liturgie de Vatican II. Esquisse historique." *La Maison-Dieu* 157 (1984): 33–52.

_____. "Langues et livres liturgiques." *La Maison-Dieu* 162 (1985): 11–22.

_____. "L'Histoire de la réforme liturgique à travers le témoignage de Mgr Annibale Bugnini." *La Maison-Dieu* 162 (1985): 125–55.

_____. "La réforme liturgique de Vatican II." *Les Quatre fleuves*, 21–22 (1985): 81–94.

_____. "La constitution liturgique et sa place dans l'œuvre de Vatican II." In *Le deuxième Concile du Vatican (1959–1965). Actes du colloque: Rome 28–30 mai 1986*, 497–509. Rome: Ecole Française de Rome, 1989.

_____. *Mirabile laudis canticum. Mélanges liturgiques, études historiques, portraits de liturgistes*. Rome: Centro Liturgico Vincenziano–Edizioni Liturgiche, 1991.

_____. "Le Mouvement liturgique en France de la fin du XIXe siècle à la veille du IIe Concile du Vatican." *Bulletin de littérature ecclésiastique* 96 (1995): 259–273.

Melloni, Alberto. "Tensioni e timori nella preparazione del Vatican II. La *Veterum sapientia* di Giovanni XXIII (22 febbraio 1962)." *Cristianesimo nella storia* 11.2 (June 1990): 275–307.

Nocent, Adrien. *Le Renouveau liturgique. Une relecture*. Paris: Beauchesne, 1993. Eng. ed.: *A Rereading of the Renewed Liturgy*. Trans. Mary M. Misrahi. Collegeville, MN: Liturgical Press, 1994.

The Ottaviani Intervention: Short Critical Study of the New Order of Mass, By Alfredo Cardinal Ottaviani, Antonio Cardinal Bacci, A Group of Theologians. Trans. Anthony Cekada. Rockford, IL: TAN Books and Publishers, 1992; new ed., West Chester, OH: Philothea Press.

Oury, Guy. *La Messe de S. Pie V à Paul VI*. Solesmes: Abbaye Saint-Pierre de Solesmes, 1975.

_____. "Paul VI et la réforme liturgique." *Esprit et Vie*, 17 November 1977: 620–22 and 1 Decembre 1977: 649–54.

Paiono, Maria. *Liturgia e società nel Novecento. Percorsi del movimento liturgico di fronte ai processi di secolarizzazione*. Rome: Edizioni di Storia e letteratura, 2000.

Paul VI et la modernité dans l'Église: Actes du colloque organisé par l'École française de Rome (Rome 2–4 juin 1983). Rome: École française de Rome, 1984.

Reid, Alcuin. *The Organic Development of the Liturgy: the Principles of Liturgical Reform and their Relation to the Twentieth-Century Liturgical Movement Prior to the Second Vatican Council.* 2nd ed. San Francisco: Ignatius Press, 2005.

Roguet, Aimon-Marie. *On nous change la religion!* Paris: Cerf, 1959.

————. "Le Centre de Pastorale Liturgique." In *Mens concordat voci. Mélanges offerts à Mgr Martimort,* 371–80. Paris: Desclée, 1983.

Le Rôle de G.-B. Montini-Paul VI dans la réforme liturgique: Actes des Journées d'études de Louvain-la-Neuve, 17 octobre 1984. Brescia: Pubblicazioni dell'Istituto Paolo VI, 1987.

Schmidt, H. "Le renouveau liturgique. Remarques et perspectives." *Nouvelle Revue Théologique* 88.8 (1966): 807–29.

Solaberrieta, Benoît-Marie. *Aimé-Georges Martimort. Un promoteur du Mouvement liturgique (1941–1962).* Paris: Cerf, 2011.

Stickler, Alfons. *Témoignage d'un expert au Concile.* Paris: C.I.E.L., 2000.

Other Works Consulted

Alberigo, Giuseppe and Joseph A. Komonchak, eds. *History of Vatican II.* 5 vols. Leuven: Peeters and Maryknoll: Orbis, 1995–2006.

Buonasorte, Nicla, ed. *Araldo del Vangelo. Studi sull'episcopato e sull'archivio di Giacomo Lercaro a Bologna, 1952–1968.* Bologna: Il Mulino, 2004.

Caprile, Giovanni. *Il Concilio Vaticano II.* 6 vols. Rome: Edizioni "La Civiltà Cattolica," 1966–1969.

Chiron, Yves. *Paul VI. Le Pape écartelé.* 2nd ed. Versailles: Via Romana, 2008.

Fesquet, Henri. *Le journal du premier Synode catholique.* Paris: Robert Morel Éditeur, 1967.

Hebblethwaite, Peter. *John XXIII: Shepherd of the Modern World.* Garden City, NJ: Doubleday, 1985.

Onofri, Nazario Sauro. *Le due anime del cardinale Lercaro.* Bologne: Capelli Editore, 1987.

Ratzinger, Joseph. *Milestones: Memoirs, 1927–1977.* San Francisco: Ignatius Press, 1998.

Zenger, Erich. *A God of Vengeance? Understanding the Psalms of Divine Wrath.* Louisville: Westminster John Knox Press, 1996.

INDEX OF NAMES

Index of Names

Index of Names

About the Author

Yves CHIRON, born in the Gard (Southern France) in 1960, obtained his degree in advanced studies in the History of Religions and Religious Anthropology at the University of Paris IV. After writing an authoritative biography of Edmund Burke, he turned his attention to modern Church history and has written biographies of Pius IX, Pius X, Pius XI, and Paul VI as well as works on the process of beatification and canonization. He lives in a small village in the Vendée.

CPSIA information can be obtained
at www.ICGtesting.com
Printed in the USA
LVHW030859040319
609386LV00007B/74/P